'Remember when'

- memories of Yesteryear

by Iris Roderick Thomas

OLD BAKEHOUSE PUBLICATIONS

© Iris Roderick Thomas

First published December 1993

The right of Iris Roderick Thomas to
be identified as author of this work has been
asserted in accordance with sections 77 and 78 of
the Copyright Designs and Patents Act 1988.

ISBN 1 874538 20 4

Published in the U.K. by
Old Bakehouse Publications
Church Street,
Abertillery, Gwent. NP3 1EA
Telephone: 0495 212600   Fax: 0495 216222
and
Supported by
South East Wales Arts Association

Made and printed in U.K.
by J.R. Davies (Printers) Ltd.

What a wonderful, imaginative idea!, though it should not come as any surprise that it comes from a writer of Iris Thomas' personality and character. Her previous writing has demonstrated a fine feeling for people and character and a deeply rooted commitment to the community.

Nostalgia and memories are part of the fabric of the community. They help to explain who we were and why we are what we are. They have an intrinsic value. They give pleasure and even sometimes pain but always give meaning to a person's life. A collection of those memories gives meaning to a community.

Historians have increasingly turned to 'oral history' to capture that which the records and the written word cannot really convey. Oral history often provides the human dimension to events. Naturally and inevitably memory is flawed. It does 'play tricks' but the flaws and 'tricks' can be as revealing as what might actually have happened.

Iris Thomas has chosen to convert the oral history of some of our oldest residents into this finely written account - Remember When?

This compilation of recollections confirms what we know. The very distinctive character of our communities has bred a host of distinctive individuals! They go together.

I have long ceased to be amazed, during my periodic visits to our residential homes, at the memory, knowledge and clear insights of our oldest residents. Many a time I have been humbled by the simple, clear perceptions the residents have of contemporary politics or economics and perceptions derived from knowledge and experience of life. We ignore such experience at our peril.

We all know 'characters' in our midst. Iris Thomas, with the love and joy which exudes from all her writing helps to capture them for us, and for posterity.

Ted Rowlands M.P.

HOUSE OF COMMONS

Ted Rowlands M.P.

3

Observations by the Author

Having carefully observed many young people born into this generation. I am somewhat perturbed to find a common denominator existing in both sexes namely an impression of intense pressure resting heavily on unprepared shoulders. I find the exact opposite existing with elderly citizens having survived the alloted span of three score years and ten.

This strange phenomena impells me to believe that whatever one feels, old at twenty or young at ninety depends to a large extent on a state of mind. Naturally we are well aware there are many exceptions to the rule, such as mental problems beyond our control, traumatic experiences that upset the equilibrium or unfortunately the sad diagnoses of terminal illness.

Each Monday afternoon, for a number of glorious weeks, I have been highly privileged to spend two hours at each of four Residential Homes in Merthyr Tydfil and the super new Home at Aberdare. All these homes are under the Mid. Glamorgan Social Service Authority and cannot be faulted for the care and attention given to the residents residing within each home.

It has proven to be an education on the constant care and heartfelt love shown to each of our senior citizens residing in one or other of the homes. The officers and staff are to be commended for a job well done and after forty weeks of experiencing life in the Residential Homes I was proud to be accepted as part of each family.

Evergreen memories related in a clear coherent manner going back ninety years in many cases, made the workshops interesting and informative and more so because all those participating were eager to join in the discussions. In general, the outlook of each individual was refreshing, their recollections phenomenal, and their company an unforgettable joy.

Three of the homes, namely Lysfaen, Sandbrook House, and Tegfan, have an interesting history which I am sure the reader will enjoy reading. The other establishments included in my account, are purpose built without a previous history for me to research.

Join with me in reliving precious moments dating back to 1893, 1895, 1896 and 1897 when Mary Edith Davies, Violet Jones, Aaron Roberts, Stanley and Lena Daniels were born into a way of life so different that this modern era with its decimal currency, Hi-Tech, and labour saving devices. Strange space age inventions that will never cease to be a source of mystery and confusion to most senior citizens. Maybe these memories recorded for posterity, will rekindle long forgotten stories related by your parents or grandparents. Times wistfully referred to as 'The Good Old Days', which somehow pale on a more thorough investigation, leaving room for speculation to the contrary.

Nevertheless, it is delightful to sit back and lose oneself in a world of eager aspirations. To listen to a wealth of information relating to past decades. Their moments of untold happiness, or moments of intense sadness, through which each of these lovely people have survived with courage and dignity to tell the tale.

Iris Roderick Thomas

Contents

Llysfaen Residential Home, Cefn Coed

Courtesy: Meirion Davies

Marged Elin with her grandson.

The History of Llysfaen

While researching into the history of Llysfaen Home for the Elderly, I became absolutely captivated by the old lady who once occupied the land prior to the site being bought by the Local Authority. After thoughful deliberation, I decided to acquaint the reader with the fascinating tale I pieced together from two separate accounts. The first account was drawn from memory and related by Jessie Mainwaring a resident in Llysfaen Home, the second was handed down through the family line to the granddaughter of this extraordinary character.

Margaret Lewis born in 1847 was the eldest and only surviving

8

daughter of William and Elinor Harris. From infancy, Marged Elin, the name she was known by to family and villagers, proved to be a strong willed individual, and with the passing of time, became one of those fascinating personages who was part and parcel of a past decade.

As a young girl Marged Elin learned her trade at the sewing machine and not being the kind to let the grass grow under her feet, plus having a keen eye for business, was soon busy sewing moleskin trousers for employees at the Iron Works and colliers in the pits.

The village of Cefn Coed was a close knit community, and it appears the inhabitants considered it a disgrace to marry anyone living beyond the set boundary of Cefn Bridge. Consequently, owing to this custom most of the villagers were related in one way or another. So it came to pass in keeping with tradition, that Marged Elin at twenty two years of age, married John Lewis a relative from another branch of the same family. The Harris family were staunch Unitarians. Anyone interested can find the graves of both her parents and brother in Hen Dy Cwrdd graveyard. Margaret and John were wed in Vaynor National School, Pontsticill owing to the Church being closed for some specific reason. The happy couple were blessed with no less than eleven children, eight of whom survived to a ripe old age.

Garreg Fawr where Llysfaen now stands, was first leased by Elinor Harris from the Crawshay brothers but on her mother's death, Marged Elin took over the farm and kept it going by sheer grit and hard work. At daybreak when most people were still fast asleep, this industrious woman would be out in the field rounding up the cows ready for milking. Mechanical machines were things to come, so hand milking had to be done early enough to get the warm fresh milk to the villagers in time for breakfast. Warming both hands by rubbing them together, Marged Elin sat hour after hour in the beast house, stopping only to move her three legged stool and position the milking pail under the next udder. This old lady was one of the last women to walk the unpaved streets of Cefn Coed y Cymmer carrying a can of milk on her head.

The can rested on a circle of material known as a 'Torchan', which beside supporting the can also protected the head. Never ever would our unique character be seen without two sheep dogs following behind and each Sunday the villagers would shake their heads in despair as Marged Elin made her way to St. John's Church with the collies running behind. Blindly ignoring forbidding looks from clergy and laity, after settling herself in pew 21, she'd noisily shoo the dogs under the wooden seat.

'Not even the Rector had enough gumption to tackle grandmother.

She was a law unto herself, fearful of neither man or beast, so the dogs remained in church until the service was over.'

Many senior residents I had the good fortune to converse with during my weeks of research, remember clearly the familiar figure dressed from head to toe in black, as she went from door to door, measuring out penny or halfpenny worth of fresh warm milk.

Beside cows, there were ducks, chickens, and geese on the small holding, so produce such as butter, poultry and eggs were for sale. Anyone upsetting the strong minded old woman was in for a rough time and it was nothing unusual to hear her high pitched voice shouting the odds after an embarrassed offender.

In stature Marged Elin was small with a sharp face and black hair drawn back severely from a centre parting. A long black dress, buttoned from neck to waist, reached to her feet and it was only when she bent that a pair of black laced knee high boots were visible. A black Welsh bonnet covered her head whatever the season, but on raw wintery days, a black cape was thrown over the frail shoulders. Indeed it was this overall black garb that gave credence to the unshakable belief that little old ladies dressed this way were in reality evil witches waiting to steal naughty children from their parents.

John Lewis who died twenty one years before his wife, was the conductor of the Welsh Church Choir but music was the least of Marged Elin's priorities with the small holding demanding every moment of her time. In contrast to their mother, all the children had excellent voices and became involved in musical circles or local choirs.

A week before the Christmas of 1922 when snow lay thick on the ground, Marged Elin died and a horse drawn hearse came to carry her remains to Vaynor Church. The horses failed to get down the narrow lane leading to the graveyard, so the coffin was transferred to a brewery dray delivering beer to the Church Tavern. It must have been a strange sight to see the chief mourners and the entire inhabitants of Cefn Coed walking slowly behind the brewery dray.

At this point in our discussion, Mrs. Maisie Gough remarked, 'Grandmother would have hit the ceiling if she knew what was happening, somebody would have felt the brunt of her tongue, and that's for sure'.

A most interesting and mysterious feature of the family home is a well in the garden that never runs dry or ices over. During frosty weather or in extreme conditions clouds of steam rise from the well and the water on testing is quite warm.

Mrs. Jones Penrhythin bought the ground where the farm was situated and later sold it to Brecon County Council. In September 1966 it was purpose built as a Home for the Elderly. The first residents at Llysfaen were two sisters, Mrs. Louise Powell and Miss Daisy Moseley. Groceries and provisions were supplied seven days a week by John Owens the local grocer.

The first 'Matron' as officers were then called, lived in the downstair flat. Residents entering the home at that time were mostly able bodied, so night staff were not required. Gradually with the admission of residents less able to cope without help during the night one helper was employed, to be shortly followed by a second and third.

In 1974 when Cefn Coed became part of Mid. Glamorgan instead of Breconshire, Llysfaen was sold to Mid. Glamorgan County Council. To date, there are 15 residents at the home, 3 full time and 4 part time care assistants, a cook, her relief and a gardener employed during day time. At night there are four night staff. All staff including casual workers are under the capable supervision of Mrs. Marilyn Bracegirdle, the Officer in Charge of both Llysfaen and Sandbrook House.

Llysfaen is an active Home where residents enjoy a wide variety of entertainment. Fund raising functions make it possible for trips to places of interest, surplus money is put to a good use by way of needed equipment or some other scheme to benefit the residents.

In fact Llysfaen sums up what we mean by HOME.

Kate Kelly
born 9th August, 1902

Kate was the eldest of six children, three boys and three girls. They lived in Rhymney where their father Dennis Carey worked for a meagre £3.9s weekly in the local pit. The money didn't go far with a wife and six hungry mouths to feed so in order to increase the budget, Dennis kept chickens, ducks and pigs on the 'small holding', which was left for his wife Emily to look after. To be truthful, the small holding was a spare plot of ground at the rear of their house in High Street but it sounded very grand to the children. Calamity struck the family when the pit closed, with no money to provide food, the chickens, ducks and pigs were put up for sale.

Kate recalls the stock being sold to a farmer. Before taking the pigs, he ringed each one in the nose, dragged the squealing animals down the back lane and bundled them into a cart, while Kate and her sisters with tear stained faces looked on in horror.

Feeding the chickens. *Courtesy: S.P. Thompson*

The family moved from Rhymney to Wellington Street, Merthyr in the hope of finding work for Kate's father. Fortunately there was a vacancy at Castle Pit so they settled down happily in their new environment. When Kate was 12 years old, the family moved to Clare Street where daily milk was delivered by a one eyed milkman. He was a chatty fellow who wore plimsoles Summer and Winter. Because of this he was nicknamed Dai Dabs. Kate remembers him telling her mother he was sailing on the 14th of September in the British White Star Liner Titanic. Later they heard the terrible news that the supposedly unsinkable ship had struck an iceberg on the second day of her maiden voyage off the Grand Banks of Newfoundland. Poor Dai Dabs was counted among the 1513 passengers who perished on September 15th 1912, a tragic day for his grief stricken family. A day to remember in Great Sea Disasters.

Three of Kate's friends earned pocket money by helping their mum clean the gallery of Park Baptist Chapel each week. One afternoon when Kate was playing with the girls, their mother Mrs. Ward, offered Kate sixpence pocket money to help with the cleaning. For almost seven months Kate worked alongside the Ward family, until her hands and knees were red raw from scrubbing planks and stone floors.

In time word reached Miss Gertie Wills via a 'clecker-box', that one of her pupils was seen working for the opposition.

'Kate is scrubbing floors in Park Chapel and they are Welsh Baptist Miss Wills'.

When Kate turned up for class the following morning Miss Wills was ready with the cancer cane.

'You wicked girl, what is a Catholic girl doing in a Welsh Baptist Chapel?' The teacher was positively jumping up and down with temper.

'I was only helping to keep it clean, Miss'.

'Hold out both hands, this will teach you to keep out of Park Chapel with pagan teachings', screamed Miss Wills applying the cane without mercy.

This was also the time when Kate along with four other Catholic girls were picked to go to Buckingham Palace where George V and Queen Mary were residing. On arriving their excitement was short lived. The five vacancies for kitchen maids had already been allocated.

The Catholic Church Priest was forever on the look out for good positions for his young flock and when a request was received from the Factory Owner of Dunlop Tyres for a kitchen maid, Kate then 14, was sent to Wimbledon. This time she was lucky. The following Monday, tired out from an endless train journey, she arrived at

The Family re-union. *Courtesy: S.P. Thompson*

Highfield House with a good conduct reference and a shabby portmanteau. Her Mistress was the daughter of a Welsh vicar, who changed her religion to marry the wealthy Honourable Mr. Hayward.

The entire staff were Catholic, with the exception of the two older maids, Mrs. Hayward brought with her from Llantwit Major.

The Haywards had six children, two older sons at boarding school and four younger children cared for by Nanny, Nurse Bradock and a capable young assistant.

Within two years Kate worked her way up to parlour maid and many times was chosen to accompany her Mistress at grand functions and garden parties held by influential business people or members of the gentry.

'I remember sitting near Queen Mary on many occasions when Mrs. Hayward attended Wimbledon Court during the tennis season. The Royals were often present at the garden parties and never left without saying a few words to Mrs. Hayward. Of course I was ordered to keep well out of sight but not too far away to be out of earshot of my Mistress'.

Kate recalls the memorable occasion when Master Valentino the eldest son, was accepted at a college in Yorkshire. Mr. Hayward was pleased as Punch and very excited and asked the housekeeper to gather the staff together in the library.

Christmas - When the staff let their hair down. *Courtesy: S.P. Thompson*

'We were each given a glass of champagne to celebrate the event and that evening the Master held a party in the grounds of Highfield House followed by a firework display'.

It was a common practice for people of the same background to

15

move into another person's residence while the family went overseas or on vacation. Such was the case each year when the Master's friend referred to as the 'Major' spent a number of weeks on his houseboat. The Great War had just commenced when orders were given to prepare for a visit to Burnt Oak Essex, the family seat of the 'Major'. All the servants accompanied the Haywards as the friends invited to reside at Highfield would be bringing their own staff. It was hard work deciding what to pack owing to our unpredictable English Summers. Mrs. Hayward left her personal packing for Kate to sort out which was quite a responsibility as well as a headache for a young girl.

The party arrived in Essex just after tea, but it was long gone midnight when bulging packing cases and tin trunks were finally unpacked and the servants allowed to go to their rooms.

'Get up quickly, cook is very ill'. Rubbing the sleep from her eyes, Kate sat up to find Bronwen white faced with fright.

'What can I do, you'd better go and wake nurse'.

'I've already called nurse, and she said we must fetch the doctor from the village at once.'

Kate dressed quickly. As the two girls ran towards the gates they noticed the sky was bright with searchlights, suddenly they heard the warning whine of air raid sirens. Though frightened sick, they were too scared to turn back before finding a doctor so they kept on running until they reached the bridge leading to the village. In a second they were surrounded by soldiers.

'What are you doing out this time of the morning? Can't you see the zeppelins overhead?'

'But we have to find a doctor', replied Kate shivering like a jelly.

'Get back home, we're expecting a raid, a doctor won't be much use if you hang about here any longer.'

Terrified the girls turned tail and raced back only to find that cook had already died from a massive heart attack.

Kate was given a months leave at the end of the war to visit her brother John who, after four years service in Egypt, contracted a tropical disease and was seriously ill. Sadly, after just one week of being together again, John took a turn for the worse and died. Kate returned to Highfield House once the funeral was over but found she wasn't happy there any longer. Those few weeks at home made her realise how much she missed her family, bravely she stuck it out a few weeks more thinking the feeling would soon pass but she became more and more homesick.

There was nothing for it but to hand in her notice and catch the next train back to good old Merthyr. Jobs came and went until Kate found work in the Belle View Hotel, Glebeland Street. One night while serving behind the bar she met a miner named George Kelly and in no time he asked her to marry him. They got married from the Belle View and came back to a splendid reception breakfast put on by the owners and staff of the Hotel without costing the newly weds a single penny.

Kate was the first resident to receive a key for a Council house on the new Keir Hardie Estate, Methyr and when she graduated to the ranks of senior citizenship, Kate was once again the first resident to be given the key to a flat in a newly completed sheltered accommodation called Greenwood Close on the same estate.

After living on the estate for 25 years the Mayor of Methyr presented her with a glass bell when Kate became the oldest resident living there.

When Kate's health deteriorated she came to Llysfaen where she is very happy. She has 9 grandchildren and one great, great grandchild. On 9th of August 1992, I was delighted to be present at Kate's ninetieth birthday held at the home. The photograph featured above is one I took of Kate and 93 year old Maggie Lewis enjoying a celebration drink.

Kate and Maggie, living it up together.

Girls together.

Just Kate.

Mary L. Morgan
born 23th September, 1905

Mary was the eldest and only girl of five children. From the tender age of three she lived with her grandparents in Merthyr Vale. Her mother Mary Jane kept in constant touch with her daughter although she lived on the opposite side of the village. During the 1914 War her father was recruited to the clerical staff and on discharge became a Civil Servant in the local Labour Exchange.

Mary's memory goes back to 1908 when she was three. She remembers a certain day when the school was turned into a soup kitchen for the village children but can't recollect what the occasion was. During my research I discovered a possible reason why the school was closed for lessons and used for the very purpose Mary mentioned.

About that time a little lad of three went missing after school and it was assummed that he'd fallen into the unfenced river running in front of the house and had drowned. The Taff was dragged for a considerable distance without any clues being furnished. Workmen from Nixon Navigation Colliery formed search parties to be joined later by 300 Volunteers of Merthyr and Merthyr Vale detachments 3rd V.B. Welsh Regiment, several members of Cefn Company of South Wales Borderers and the police. They searched the mountain sides inch by inch between Merthyr and Treharris but there was no trace of little Cromwell Davies from Taff Street, Merthyr Vale. Soup kitchens were set up in local schools to provide hot drinks for the army of volunteers and children whose parents were out searching for the missing boy.

A house to house collection was made to pay a diver to explore the deep pools hoping they held the secret of Cromwell's disappearance. Watched by 1,500 people the diver rose after each search with the same response.

'Nothing there'.

Three weeks passed during which various sightings of the boy were reported to the police. One person was certain the boy was at a gypsy camp, another said he was locked up in a house near Brecon but all leads proved a waste of time.

Finally four expert salmon fishermen complete with coracles arrived from Carmarthen to make a slow but thorough search of the Taff as far as Cardiff. Nearing the weir at Quakers Yard they cast a salmon net sweeping a hundred yards above the weir. Having completed the circle they hauled the net in, and the body of little Cromwell Davies rose slowly to the surface. At last the long search was over.

Chapel was an important part of village life when Mary was a child. Each Sunday morning accompanied by her grandparents and Auntie Martha, she walked the rough road to Saron Chapel Troedyrhiw for morning service. After dinner Mary attended Sunday School at the Welsh Baptist Chapel, Merthyr Vale and once tea was over the family once more tackled the long trek to Saron, for Evening Service.

The Annual Sunday school trip was a walk up the mountain for a picnic in Pendycae field or Pontygwaith. In later years when Mary was a young lady Sunday school picnics ceased and the children went by train to Barry Island.

Games like whip and top, hoops, or skipping were played in the middle of the road there being no fear of motor cars disturbing their play. Sometimes the children played in the coke ovens and engine house of an old level on the side of the mountain. A favourite game was mothers and fathers where dolls became babies and broken china, discarded pans, were used to decorate their pretend houses and lemonade sherbert was drunk from jam jars. No-one worried unduly about the children playing on the mountainside until dark. Indeed it was a rare thing for a child to be abducted or molested, and as for child rape, it was unheard of in the valleys back there in 1908.

Mary remembers the Aerial Flight during the working years of the colliery which crossed above the main road between Merthyr Vale and Troedyrhiw. Huge buckets carried small coal form the pit to Danyderi on the opposite side of the mountain. Mingled with the small coal were sizable lumps and it was a common sight to see families searching for coal on the mountain side.

The Infant School was just across the road from her grandparents' house. A daily ride on the lovely rocking horse helped keep the children happy and Mary spent hours making pom poms from crinkle paper of every colour ready for decorating the classrooms at Christmas. When the time came for changing schools, life became hazardous as now it was necessary to cross the colliery yard to catch a train leaving on the Rhymney line.

'I remember distinctly crawling under loaded trucks and soiling my dress with filthy black oil which kept dripping off the couplings. On reaching the station, I'd run up the steps and cross the bridge to the other side of the platform just in time to catch the school train'.

It was on the 27th October 1913 that a fierce tornado struck the Merthyr valleys. One of the most remarkable features of the storm was

Beechgrove Farm, Edwardsville after the tornado.   Courtesy: *Merthyr Public Libraries*

the sharpness of its boundaries on either side of the track. Being eight at the time Mary can remember how frightened she was.

'It was about teatime when everything went dead quiet and as it got darker the atmosphere was stifling. We all felt uneasy. Then the rain started to bucket down followed by loud crashes of thunder. The lightning was red and deep blue in turns, then I heard a sound like a noisy locomotive coming nearer and nearer.'

Devastation after tornado. *Courtesy: Merthyr Public Libraries*

The tornado passed over Merthyr Vale with little damage, but areas between Quakers Yard and Treforest were badly hit as buildings toppled, roofs were ripped off, and people blown about like rubber balls. Thomas John Harris a resident of Cilfynydd was lifted bodily into the air and found dead the following day in a field behind his back garden. Five people were killed, many injured and twenty families left homeless. It was hard to imagine that all this destruction had taken place in a few minutes.

BEECH GROVE FARM EDWARDSVILLE AFTER THE TORANDO OCTOBER 1913

A week or so before starting at the Cyfarthfa Secondary School, the Great War came to an end and Mary took part in the 1918 Victory celebrations. Dressed in Girl Guide Uniform, the girls marched round Merthyr Vale school yard singing a Girl Guide song called 'Marching on the King's Highway'. In 1922 Cyfarthfa School pupils living between Troedyrhiw and Treharris were transfered to Quakers Yard Secondary School which meant another change of schools for Mary. Her work was standard but there was one aspect she took great pleasure in, reading the scripture at morning assembly. When Saint David's day came round each year, Mary was one of the soloists chosen to sing in the presence of schoolmates, visitors and her family. In 1924 she left school having sat the Oxford School Certificate and achieved passes in Botany, English, Maths, Geography, French and Art. Mary hoped to do uncertificated teaching, making it unnecessary to attend college but replacements were few and in the end she accepted the post of pharmacist assistant in a local chemist shop. This was also the year in which her grandfather died. Thirty four years were spent at the pharmacy, resulting in Mary becoming a well known and respected member of the community.

As previously mentioned, Chapel played an important role in

Rule Brittania. A young Mary Morgan.

Mary's life. One of her earliest memories goes back to the days she walked the one and a half miles twice on Sunday to Saron Chapel Troedyrhiw with her grandparents in order to hear the Reverend J.W. Price better known as Price Saron, render Bible sermons full of the 'Hwyl'. Price Saron who was ordained in 1886, preached at the same chapel for 42 years until his death.

The Reverend Teifionydd Hughes took over but sadly, the membership of the once crowded Saron fell drastically following his death and because it was difficult to get preachers. In 1983 as there were under a dozen women attending, a closure service was inevitable. It was Calfaria Chapel from then on for Mary, who beside attending each meeting conducted her own Sunday School class. For years she faithfully fulfilled her obligation as Sunday School Superintendent but members began leaving for various reasons and not long after the minister died. On October 6th 1974 Calfaria Welsh Baptist joined with the English Baptist and a bi-lingual Baptist Church was formed. That Chapel is also demolished.

I quote Mary's words at our last interview.

'Most of my life has been centred round Chapel, Sunday school, and the Band of Hope where I was taught to read Welsh and tonic solfa with the aid of the Modulator'.

When Troedyrhiw Choir won 1st prize at Caerphilly National Eisteddfod.

She had the conductor of 'Calfaria' Merthyr Vale to thank for this added education enabling her to take part in competitive meetings between Baptist Methodist and Wesleyan chapels in the village. Mary took part in concerts, the first being 'Holiday Concert', followed by 'United Britain', 'Beauty and the Beast' followed by 'Aladdin' in 1929.

Whitsun Monday was a special day in Mary's calendar because the children she taught at morning service took part in the Treharris Cymanf. On Easter Tuesday she went to Zoar Chapel, Merthyr to sing in the Cymanfa Ganu.

A very important occasion was when Troedyrhiw Choir where Mary was a member, was asked to compete at the National Eisteddfod. Their leader was the Reverend Davies minister of Carmel Chapel and the choir was awarded first prize in the second choral at Caerphilly. They did well again the next year, this time carrying off second prize in the chief choral but unfortunately in later years, the choir was forced to disband due to lack of members. Mary joined both the Merthyr Philharmonic Choir and the Nelson Choral Society during her working years and continued with them until her retirement. Her Aunt was now old and infirm but Mary never forgot the loving care she'd received as a child. They talked for hours about the long walk to Saron Chapel and old times as Mary gently attended to Aunts' needs until the day the old lady passed peacefully away.

Mary's own health began to deteriorate and she quickly realised she must find sheltered accommodation. Having been hospitalised from time to time it was decided after discussing things with both family and a social worker that it was the only answer. She spent four years

Mary L. Morgan

at Ty Bryngoleu sheltered accomodation until her transfer to Llyswen three and a half years ago where she tries to keep as active as possible.

Religion remains Mary's greatest love so from time to time she's happy to lend a hand in organising services for the residents. Not long ago Mary was presented with a lovely sewing box from caring companions at Llyswen and makes jolly good use of it by sewing bits and pieces as a gesture of appreciation for their kindness.

Edward Summers
born 30th September, 1915

Eddy as he was called, lived with his parents, five brothers and one sister in Station Terrace, Dowlais Top. As a child he remembers most of the neccessities for every day survival such as coal, milk, bread, vegetables being delivered by horse and cart. His father who worked in South Tunnel Fochrhiw was from hard working mining stock, like his own father and grandfather before him. His mother Elvira Summers, found little time for leisure with six children to care for. Eddy remarked,

'If she wasn't in the scullery cooking, you'd find her either bent over the washing board, or busy ironing.'

When Eddy was eight he remembers his brother David having the key to the front door because it was his 21st birthday and he was old enough to take on responsibilities.

'We didn't have much money to spare', said Eddy, 'but Mam made a bit of a do for the neighbours and Dad took the men to the pub for a pint on him'. Eddy also recalls another day not long afterwards when news arrived from Bedlinog Colliery, informing the family that David had been involved in a fall. It appeared he was still alive when the rescue team freed him from the heavy timbers, but he died at the side of the mine while waiting for the medical team to arrive. Once again the neighbours were invited to tea and the men went to the pub just like they did on David's birthday but on this occasion instead of laughter there was weeping. It was a sad house for many months to come.'

'I don't think Mam ever recovered from the shock of losing our David, he was the first born and her two eyes'.

In June 1926, Mr. S.O. Davies received a telephone message informing him the Lady Astor M.P. intended visiting Merthyr and Dowlais. She intended seeing for herself the conditions under which valley workers were living. As the miners' agent, he was asked to organise a tour of the streets so Lady Astor could speak freely with residents in order to collect all the necessary information.

It so happened the Dowlais Male Voice Party were rehearsing, 'Jesus of Nazareth', by Dr. Joseph Parry that very week and as Lady Astor had expressed a desire to hear Welsh singing, it was decided to include this event in the schedule.

Lady Astor and party, accompanied by Mr. and Mrs. S.O. Davies, visited many Merthyr streets. Men, women and children, were questioned at random about their squalid living conditions and asked what reforms they wished to see in the valleys. As planned, the party called to hear the choir rehearsing. Being one of the tenors, Eddy's father had reserved seats for the family with an excellent view of the stage. It was later reported that Lady Astor and her party sat enthralled throughout the performance. Mr. S.O. Davies made the introductions mid loud cries of 'Speech, Speech', with which Lady Astor immediately complied.

'I remember how nice she was', remarked Eddy who was 11 at the time, 'she thanked the choir for their wonderful singing then got down from the stage to mingle with the audience. She asked questions like how could large families live in such little houses and how did they manage to clothe and feed the children on meagre wages'.

Eddy left Dowlais Central School at fifteen only to find his friends were going to work underground.

'Come with us Eddy', said Jim, 'we'll all be together then'.

That evening, when Eddy told his mother what he intended doing, she almost hit the roof.

'Isn't it enough to lose one son underground without another going the same way?', she cried so Eddy thought it wiser to let the matter drop.

In the end he became a delivery boy for the local grocer. When the grocer decided to reduce Eddy's wages of 5/- to half the amount, his mother told him to pack the job in. Eventually Eddy had his way and joined his school friends in Trelewis Drift. He worked in various drifts for a total of 45 years but at 60 owing to ill health he was forced to retire.

Before the Central Library, Merthyr was built, Eddy remembers an old army tank standing in St. David's Yard as a monument to the town's war effort in 1914-18. The Borough raised £1 million to help build tanks, the chief fund raiser was Seymour Berry, later known as Lord Buckland. This 'Super Tank', on display, had gone into action for the first time in 1916 and was viewed with wonder and awe by youngsters like Eddy. Later the tank was transferred to Cyfarthfa Park and placed on a plinth at the West Grove entrance. During the Second World war, the tank was used for urgently required scrap in the manufacture of upto date armaments.

The 'Super Tank' on display in St. David's Yard.　　　*Courtesy: Merthyr Public Libraries*

When Sergeant John Collins was awarded the Victoria Cross, postcards of the tank were printed and sold to Merthyr residents to celebrate his home coming as a local hero.

The 'Coal Arch', a symbolic ingress to the dark mills of industry was specially constructed as the official entrance to Dowlais Steelworks before the visit of King George V and Queen Mary on 27th June, 1912.

As such, the 'Coal Arch' never ceased to impress Eddy as a boy because it had a crown on each of the two pillars and a huge crown suspended by iron uprights across the top.

The inscription UNDERNEATH the crown reads as follows,

DUW CADW ein BRENIN a BRENHINES
which translated means
GOD KEEP our KING and QUEEN

Like most boys, young Eddy enjoyed going out with girls, but never got too serious with the flavour of the month.

'I could take or leave them, it didn't really matter one way or another.'

This proved true until the day he went to Bristol and saw the girl of his dreams.

'Well, mam, I've met the girl I want to marry', he said on returning home.

'How can you think of marrying, when I need you to look after me', was the reply he received.

And that proved to be that. Eddy never tried to contact his love again. Instead, he persuaded himself that by working extra shifts there'd be no time to brood over what might have been. So from then

Strike March passing General Hospital.

on it was a bed to work existance for Eddy until Beryl became a distant memory. Like a dutiful son, each pay day he handed over his pay packet to his mother. In return he received enough pocket money to buy a few pints or go to the pictures at weekends. The years slipped quickly by and with them went his aspirations of settling down with a wife and family of his own.

Eddy's health began to fail so he took early retirement. For the first time in his life now his mother was gone, he was free to do his own thing. Unfortunately his condition deteriorated and was unable to cope alone. In 1990 he joined the residents at Llyswen.

Oddly enough, it was here that Eddy discovered a talent never exploited. One day during a concert at the home, a singer asked for a volunteer to join him in a sing a long and our Eddy got up for a lark. He astonished the residents as well as the soloist when he started to sing, since that day he frequently entertains staff and his loving companions at the home. His repertoire includes three favourite songs in order of merit;

Have I told you lately that I love you

My Mother's Birthday

Sixty Three Candles

There's one photograph that Eddy cherishes above all other. It shows the well known soloist and Eddy singing together into a microphone.

On completion of my workshops at Llysfaen, I felt really privileged when Eddy sang his favourite song especially for me. Another lovely memory for my own treasure chest.

Edward Summers

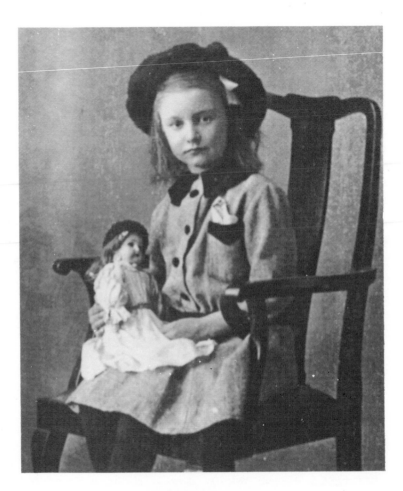

Megan Lewis
born 20th September, 1909

Megan Morgan was the third and last child born to David Morgan and his second wife Margaret who was then thirty nine years old. To be nearing forty was considered a dangerous age for child bearing but nevertheless Margaret was anxious to give her two boys 11 year old Emrys and 9 year old Henry a little sister before it was too late. The baby was born one chilly November day in 1909 and to everyones delight, was a plump healthy girl.

Their happiness at having a sister was shattered when the mother they obviously adored, failed to recover from the birth and in less than six weeks was dead.

Many years later when Megan was sorting out books belonging to her father, she came across an old diary. Turning the pages she read the words quoted below.

Nov. 29 1909   Maggy was delivered of a bouncing baby girl.

Dec. 25 1909   Maggy passed away quietly this morning, don't know what to say to my boys, when they're expecting Santa Claus to come with presents.

Many years later, Megan learned from her father that the Salvation Army were playing carols outside the house that Christmas morning as her mother lay dying. At the precise moment of death, the choir began singing, 'O Come All Ye Faithful'.

'From that day on', remarked her father, 'I have never been able to hear that carol without reliving the agony of that tragic morning.'

For the second time in twelve years David Morgan became a widower. Margaret Ann, the daughter of his first marriage was fifteen years old when her half sister Megan was born. The older girl took a training course at Merthyr Infirmary and on becoming a S.R.N., accepted the post of district nurse in Aberaeron.

Slowly, David who was a Credit Draper by trade, started putting his life in order after his traumatic experience and got married for the third time to a lady from a rural village in Cardigan. One very special day when Megan was six, her stepmother said they were going to Wesley Chapel after lunch.

'I thought this was odd because as a family we all attended Bethesda, but I got ready in plenty of time like Mama told me'.

On arriving at Wesley Chapel, Megan soon discovered the reason for their visit. The Great War of 1914 hadn't long started and it was difficult to get enough eggs to supply the soldiers. An appeal had been launched by the Mayor, asking Merthyr residents to bring their surplus eggs to the chapel where they'd be collected and taken to the nearest barracks. Being from the country, Megan's stepmother had filled a large basket with fresh brown eggs and decorated the handle with ribbons and crepe. The Chapel was heaving with people bringing whatever eggs they could or in most cases could not spare. Like Megan's stepmother, most of the women had wrapped pretty paper round their baskets, and the more artistic among them, had painted scenes or messages of good luck on the eggs.

'They were too pretty to eat', said Megan as she recalled the occasion.

Before the baskets were handed to the minister, the children were asked to write their names and addresses on every egg contributed by their mothers. Very soon letters addressed to Miss Megan Morgan, Thomas Street, Merthyr began arriving from grateful soldiers. Those simple letters became her most cherished and treasured possession as a child and were kept safely tucked away long after the War had ended.

Another happy memory from the old days was dancing to the hurdy gurdy on the street corner. Megan recalls lifting her skirt high above her knees like the other girls and dancing the polka down the length of the street. It was rumoured years later, that the men in charge of the hurdy gurdy were in fact German spies gathering information and military secrets for their Fatherland. This was never confirmed as being true, half true or merely fabrication.

The children were quite old enough to care for themselves by now, leaving David Morgan time to write poetry and compose music. His work was good enough to earn him the title of Bard and as recently as August 1992, Megan handed her father's poetic works to a representative of the National Library of Wales. A letter of acknowledgement and grateful thanks has since been received by Megan.

Emrys and Henry were now old enough to join the services and chose the Merchant Navy. Harry, the name he was called at home, was on the first P & O British Liner to be torpedoed in the Mediterranean and when the ship was struck he happened to be in the bath. The warning sounded abandon ship, so grabbing his service coat Harry raced for the lifeboat. Hours later he was picked up by the City of Marseilles a ship taking missionaries to India. Imagine his surprise when Aranwen Evans reknowned for her missionary work came over to chat with him.

'Where are you from?', she asked.

'South Wales ma'm', Harry replied.

'What part of South Wales?', Aranwen wanted to know.

'Merthyr Tydfil'.

'And where in Merthyr do you live?'

'Thomas Street'.

Aranwen smiled, 'It's a small world, I'm from West Grove'.

Both Harry and Emrys survived the 1914 war without mishap but during the Second World War Emrys then living at St. David's, became Chief Engineer for Shell Oil. However, the boat taking him to his destination was torpedoed but unlike Harry who after suffering the same fate in 1914, was fortunate enough to be picked up by a passing ship, poor Emrys had no such luck. In due course his wife Edna received the customary telegram stating Emrys was missing and presumed killed. His body was never retrieved from the sea.

At the age of ten Megan not only recited at school and in Cymanfa

Ganu but went each Friday to Cymru Geiddion at Pontmorlais vestry to hear her father lecture in Welsh on Merthyr Musicians. As a result of the lectures David Morgan was asked by Merthyr Tydfil Authority to write a book on Music and Musicians in Merthyr, with the added task of translating it from Welsh into English. The book can still be found in many libraries throughout the country and Mr. John Downey reference librarian at Merthyr Central Library, kindly photocopied a double spread for the readers perusal.

MUSIC AND MUSICIANS
OF MERTHYR AND
DISTRICT

Together with a LIST
OF EISTEDDFODAU
to the year 1901

BY

DAVID MORGANS
(Cerddwyson)

Merthyr Tydfil
H. W. Southey & Sons Ltd., *Merthyr Express*, Glebeland Street

1922

Megan did well at school and decided to be a teacher but before entering college all students were obliged to do one year training locally, so at seventeen she was allocated to Queen's Road School to experience what teaching was about. She had barely settled in when the Head Mistress, asked Megan if she was willing to take a class on her own while the teacher in charge was off sick.

'I was really nervous', said Megan, 'but Mrs. Morgan knowing I'd been accepted at Swansea Training College for Teachers, said the experience I'd gain would be beneficial'.

Megan decided to give it a try and enjoyed being teacher to a class of pupils not all that much younger then herself. Many incidents from that so memorable term are clearly outlined in her mind. Turning one day from the blackboard, she noticed a little girl clicking her nails together.

'Whatever are you doing Gladys?', she asked.

The class where Megan first experienced the joys of teaching.

'Killing fleas Miss'.

Megan was shocked. Putting the top girl in charge of the class she ran to fetch Mrs. Morgan who accompanied her back to the classroom where Gladys was busy killing fleas. During that time, Queens Road was the only school able to boast a Domestic Unit, to where Gladys was speedily taken and swiftly plunged into a bath containing carbolic disinfectant. The staff, feeling sorry for the child, clubbed together to replace the flea infested clothes that had to be burned in the classroom stove. Not many days later, Gladys, turned up in old clothes handed down from an elder sister, because Bronwen James, her mother, had sold the new garments to buy drink for her husband.

Gladys James was an extraordinarily pretty girl. For that reason Megan chose her to play the part of Wendy Darling in a one act version of Peter Pan written by herself.

'Don't forget to bring your nightgown or pyjamas for the bedroom scene Gladys', said Megan on rehearsal afternoon.

'I haven't got a nightgown or pyjamas, I wear my old dress or petticoat in bed, or nothing at all, Miss Morgan'.

One evening after chapel Megan and her father called to see a couple of straight laced old ladies who kept a jam jar on their window sill filled with a yellowy liquid alive with some kind of small wriggling insects. On this particular night they were invited to taste a glass of Bees Wine, and ended up drunk as cootes. Each day the jar was topped up with sugared water, left to ferment in the sunlight then bottled and corked.

'I was horrified to find out later that the wriggling mass inside the jam jar, were trapped bees trying to get out'. Megan shuddered at the thought.

All students during the training year, went back to their own school for a day each week, which in Megan's case happened to be Merthyr Intermediate School. On the particular day I refer to, a classmate mentioned to Megan about the teacher taking the French Class.

'Have you seen him yet, Megan?, he's a real cracker.'

In fact, he too was a student standing in for Miss Thomas who happened to be on leave of absence.

Later that same afternoon Megan bumped into him in the corridor, smiling, he quickly apologised. Little did Megan realise at the time, she was looking at her future husband.

There were no vacancies in Merthyr for teachers when Megan left college therefore she was obliged to take a post in Broadstairs. One day while on vacation she met a young man called Lewis Lewis.

'Don't you remember me Megan?', he asked after they'd chatted a while.

'No, I can't say I do'.

'I remember you very well'.

Megan had no recollection of ever seeing him before in her life. He smiled.

'You bumped into me at the County School when I was acting French Master'.

Of course they fell in love, and not long afterwards Megan applied for a post at Dowlais Central School and was successful. Later she took a post at Queens Road School where she had began her career.

In 1935 Megan and Lewis were married at Bethesda Chapel and moved into Pentwyn Villas where their son Geoffrey and daughter Dilys were born. Both children went to Cambridge, Geoffrey to St. John's College, and Dilys to Homerton College. Dilys taught at Watford for a while, Geoffrey trained to be an anaesthetist.

Megan Lewis

Megan is proud of her children but the highlight of her life was on the day Geoffrey and his bride were married at St. Paul's Cathedral, London.

'It was a shame Lewis wasn't there beside me to share my happiness, still I must be thankful he lived long enough to see both our children receive their Cap and Gown at the passing out ceremony in Cambridge. That special day when I walked the length of St. Paul's aisle behind my son and his bride will remain in my memory for ever. I felt like a queen as photographers rushed to take our photos. Later, I was proud as Punch, to see the wedding group featured in a famous society magazine.

Wonderful memories and albums of photographs keep Megan contented at Llysfaen where she enjoys the company of other ladies who like herself, reminisce frequently on the good old days back there.

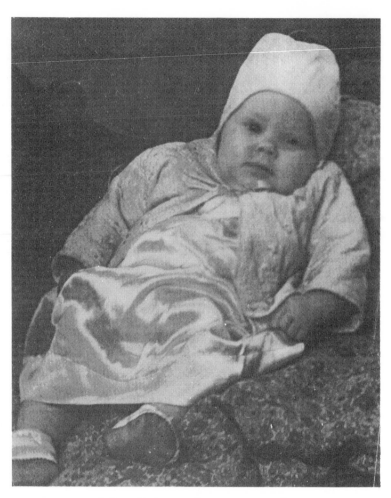

Magdalene Strangward
born 5th June, 1912

Magdalene was one of two girls and two boys born to Annie May and William James Jones, or Jas as he was called by family, friends and neighbours. Their house was a centre for musical evenings because Jas had inherited the remarkable talent known as playing by ear. Classics, ballads, and popular songs of the decade were included in his repertoire. Even those who learned to read music in the authentic way had to admit Jas was a superb pianist.

At the tender age of four or five Magdalene used to creep into the front parlour when no one was watching, remove the cloth draped over the piano and tinkle the keys. It seemed sensible to cover the piano for fear of dust getting into the strings, but Magdalene never could fathom out the reason for wrapping old stockings around the legs of the piano and family table. Once she was so busy trying to make up a tune, she failed to hear footsteps coming towards her. The next thing she heard was the sound of the sea in her earhole, a frequent after effect from having one's ears boxed.

Although Jas was easy going with the children, Annie May was a different kettle of fish. Her attitude to life was almost purotan, she'd stand no nonsense from Jas or the children under any circumstances. In line with her general outlook, even music fell into two catogories. Popular ballads like In A Monastery Garden, Bless This House, Oh, Sweet Mystery of Life, Trees and depressing hymns fell into the first category, while comic or modern tunes were labelled RUBBISH.

You can well imagine her horror one evening when the family were entertaining guests to hear Magdalene break all tradition by singing a favourite music hall ditty. Worse still, neighbours on both sides, hearing the song through their open windows, decided to join Magdalene in the well known chorus of;

'Joshua, Joshua, why don't you call and see Papa,

He'd be pleased I know, that you're my best Beau,

Joshua, Joshua, nicer than lemon squash you are,

Oh by gosh you are, Joshua, Joshua'.

When the clapping subsided, Annie May thoroughly disgusted by the choice of song, took Jas to one side.

'I demand you reprimand her here and now or there'll be hell to play'

To which Jas replied, 'There's nothing to say, your face said it all'.

Magdalene was a pupil at Cefn Infant and Junior School. Like all children she had a favourite teacher, this particular teacher was Miss Evans, Lower Vaynor Road who took charge of Standard 7. Although considerably older than most of the staff, she was by far the most popular teacher in the school. Her kind and considerate manner to pupils was probably the reason for her popularity during a period when many teachers were strict and straight laced with the children.

If correction in either scholastics or deportment was necessary, Miss Evans tackled it in a manner so as not to belittle the child or encourage other pupils to poke fun afterwards.

While Magdalene loved Miss Evans to distraction, the opposite was true regarding Mrs. Knox whom she both hated and feared with every fibre of her being. The main cause for Magdalene's dislike stemmed from the liberal way Mrs. Knox used the cancer cane when punishment was meted out. Indeed one could say the lady was an

When shoes were the princely sum of 10 shillings and 11 pennies.

expert in that department. She cared little about the gender of an offender, the same pressure was applied to girls and boys alike, the cane was applied without mercy.

One Winter morning the classroom stove refused to light because the pipe was clogged. Mrs. Knox sent at once for Magdalene's aunt who was employed as a cleaner. Beside keeping the classrooms tidy, her duties included lighting and seeing to the stoves. Being most interested in what her aunt was doing, young Magdalene, when called out to read in front of the class, missed out a whole page of the story. Mrs. Knox was furious. Picking up the cane, she brought it down on the little girl's fingers with all the force she could muster, making Magdalene cry out in pain.

Instead of saying nothing which most domestics would have done under the same circumstances, Magdalene's aunt, filthy dirty from clearing the blockage, grabbed the teacher and began shaking her backwards and forward as if she were a rag doll. Mrs. Knox was terrified as the cleaner screamed out,

'Apologise to my niece or I'll shake the living daylight from you'.

The children clapped and cheered on hearing their teacher apologise to a pupil. Much worse for Miss Knox, were the secret smiles and sly nudges when later, she joined her colleagues in the staff room. If anyone had their come uppance that day, it was poor Mrs. Knox. Needless to say, the little girl was never forgiven for the indignity and loss of face silently borne by the teacher.

On leaving school her mother begged Magdalene to do anything rather than go into service but Magdalene turned a deaf ear. At sixteen she went to work for John John in his grocery stores at Brecon Road for the handsome wage of five shillings weekly. Magdalene later became a housekeeper for the John family and her salary was increased to 25/- (125p) a week.

During the war she worked in an ammunition factory and often talks about the blackout and windows taped with criss cross brown paper to prevent the glass flying if an air raid occured.

Magdalene married Bill Strangward late in life but unfortunately he died shortly afterwards. There were no children from the union so she decided to go home to her mother and sister. They were looking for a cook at Llysfaen and Magdalene applied for the vacant position. Having been accepted, she worked there until her retirement. At long last, Magdalene had time on her hands to do the one thing she'd dreamed of doing, during her busy years as cook in Llysfaen.

'I became a member of both the Philharmonic and Gurnos Ladies choirs'.

DOWLAIS LADIES CHOIR, 1934

The Dowlais Choir of which Magdalene belonged.

Singing had given her great pleasure as a child but what she'd felt then couldn't compare with the joy she now experienced. It not only gave meaning to what otherwise may have become a lonely existence, but brought many new friends into her life.

Sadly, Magdalene suffered a slight stroke in 1989 and was admitted to hospital. On being discharged, she returned once more to Llysfaen Home where she'd spent so many happy years. Circumstances were now reversed and Magdalene became a resident.

She loves going out to concerts and meals organised by Mrs. Marilyn Bracegirdle the officer in charge of Llysfaen and still keeps in touch with many members from both choirs she once belonged to.

Magdalene has never lost her love for singing, there's nothing she likes better than joining in with the choir when they come along to entertain the residents of Llysfaen from time to time.

Magdalene Strangward

Violet Sarah Jones
born 25th May, 1895

Violet was the youngest of four daughters born to Margaret and Gwilym Havard and began attending Abermorlais School at five years of age. The building was divided into the Boys School with Mr. Jenkins as Headmaster while the Girls School was in the capable hands of his sister. A long iron railing running between the sections separated the boys from the girls at playtime. Mr. and Miss Jenkins, like most Head Teachers those days, were disciplinarians down to the last letter.

The family lived on a small holding in Rhydycar so there was plenty to do when school was over. Violet's chore was to feed the chickens and clean out the pigs, certainly not the easiest of tasks. One morning, a sow jumped the stone wall of the cote and Violet chased it all along the canal bank until it was cornered in Aberdare Tunnel. By this time the child was thoroughly exhausted and far to small to drag the sow out, in fact it bit her finger so she tried to get her arms round its neck. In the end it took five men to get the runaway back to Rhydycar with little Violet bringing up the rear.

Sunday meant two visits instead of the customary three to Ynysgau Chapel because their customers had rice or other milk puddings to prepare in time for lunch. Margaret Hammond would pour the warm fresh milk from the milking bucket into the large churn and Violet would jump up beside her father on the milk cart. There were three measures with long handles hanging from the churn, the smallest for a halfpenny worth of milk, the medium for a penny worth and the pint measure for two pennies worth. The horse knew every stop on the round and when he halted outside a gate, Violet would knock the door and hand the customer's jug or basin to her father. He always added extra milk for good measure.

About the same time as Violet left school, her parents adopted a nine year old boy called Tom Griffiths and found later to their dismay that the child suffered from epilepsy. On leaving school, the Gas Board took him on as an apprentice but after a few weeks dismissed Tom saying he was a danger to both himself and the other employees. As a result he was barred from all manual work but when war broke out he was accepted for the army and when the war ended he was given a white collar job in the City Hall Cardiff.

'I could never understand why Tom was considered a danger to employees at the Gas Works but accepted in the forces without any bother', said Violet.

How the milk was delivered by Violets' father. The horse and cart above belonged to Merlin Clayton, 'The Wern Farm', Ynysfach.

Her middle sister Annie Margaret, passed high in school and went to Bangor College, her eldest sister learned her trade as a dressmaker, while Violet had no option but to stay at home as the maid of all work.

There were no washing machines or driers those days. Instead the washing was done in a zinc bath or wooden tub which was in reality a sawn in half brewers barrel with a handle cut at each side for carrying. Neither were there electric heaters for boiling water like housewives have today. Washing day was hard work as the water had first of all to be carried from an outside tap and poured into an iron boiler or galvanised bucket ready for boiling on the open fire. Filling the tub was a never ending task as bucket after bucket of boiling water was carried outside, refilled with cold water and put back on the fire to boil. Beside seeing to the water, the fire had to be stoked and kept at a constant heat or the washing would never get done. A wooden dolly was used to swish the clothes round and thump the dirt out but later on they were replaced by scrubbing boards.

Wash day at school.   *Courtesy: Merthyr Public Libraries*

'I've seen my mother starting to wash at daybreak and if it was a big wash with white sheets and other bedding, sometimes it would be dark before she finished. Everything was hung out to dry on a wire line with a prop placed in the centre of the clothes to raise them high above our heads for the wind to blow them dry. White clothes were dipped in Reckitts blue, while pillow cases, tablecloths, shirt collars, and handkerchiefs were dipped in a bowl of starch before being hung out to dry. Sheets, blankets, bedspreads and curtains were put through a hand operated mangle to remove excess water.

'Yes it was a lovely sight to see whiter than white sheets dancing overhead on the three thick wire lines that ran the length of our garden'.

Once dry, the clothes were folded and put into a big basket ready for ironing. This was a chore needing a great deal of preparation and the most hated of all household tasks.

'The washing took a day, but the ironing took forever', said Violet.

The family table was first covered with an old blanket to prevent the heat damaging the polished top. There were no plug in electric irons but heavy flat irons that were heated between the bars of the grate. Thick pads of old material were sewn together and used to remove the hot irons from the fire and a wire stand stood ready to hold the iron when not in use.

'Mam used to spit on the hot surface to test the temperature and if the moisture sizzled and spluttered the iron was hot enough. Sometimes soot or bits of coke from the fire stuck to the iron. To stop the clothes getting soiled, the iron was rubbed onto a piece of white Sunlight soap before use.

Violet Sarah Jones

A basin of cold water was also placed on the side of the table and a young member of the family damped down the stiff starched clothes by sprinkling them with water. Each damped down garment was then rolled up tight and left for the water to circulate through the material.

'It was miraculous how shiny the starched shirt collars and tablecloths were after being ironed. When Dad was going somewhere special, Mam would starch his shirt as well as the collar and every time he moved the shirt would crackle but we pretended not to hear in case he couldn't see the funny side'.

To keep house those days meant being on your feet from morning till night with little time for yourself but despite the hard work they were good old days to look back on.

Violet is a recent member of Llysfaen but like her companions is very happy there.

Residents of Llysfaen in the Day Room.

Waiting for the Workshop to commence.

Other residents observing the Workshop.

Myself, Officer Marilyn Bracegirdle, Mary, Kate, Megan, Magdalene. Eddy is the rose in the middle.

Discussing past experiences with six participants at the Workshop.

Staff and residents of Llysfaen.

We want our photo with Eddy.

We love having 'our likeness took'.

Victoria House,
Dowlais, Merthyr

Courtesy: Meirion Davies

Annie May Upham
born 5th February, 1904

Ann as she liked to be called was the eldest of three girls and two boys. Her memory is truly remarkable. She has no problems in relating events from the tender age of three onwards. Ann talked about a long gone Chapel called Shiloh in Church Street, Merthyr, where the rear rooms were used daily as a school. This is the first time reference has been made to the demolished chapel and from what I can gather, a kind of infant school was held there for children living in that area. At five Ann attended the Salvation Army School at the foot of the British Tip, and although she had to walk from the Tramroad into town and across the length of Glebeland Street, not once was she accompanied by an older person.

'You didn't need an adult to take you to school, it was quite safe to go by yourself those days. Now children have to be taken and fetched

58

home by a responsible person or goodness knows where they'd end up. You've only to watch the tele or read a newspaper to know children aren't safe anymore.'

Never was a truer word spoken.

The outside 'Lav'.

Courtesy: John A. Owen

As in most houses, the toilet, commonly called the 'Lav', was situated outside and in most cases had to be flushed manually after use. If one was fortunate enough to have a garden, the Lav could usually be found at the very bottom. In the depth of Winter when snow lay thick on the ground, it was freezing in the Lav and if that wasn't enough persecution, there'd be three or four buckets of water needed to flush the pan. On one occasion a big rat climbed up the wooden seat and Ann ran screaming to her father. Armed with a hammer and a bucket of water he threw his cap over the rat and popped it in the bucket.

'I thought it was massive before Dad drowned it, but it shrunk to nothing in the water and I felt sorry that Dad killed the poor thing.'

Ann was seven when her youngest brother was born and she was allowed to carry him downstairs for the first time. The midwife went completely mad when Ann started to descend the stairs. Snatching

Inside the water closet before demolition. *Courtesy: John A. Owen*

the baby from the little girl she screamed out;

'You can't carry a new baby down steps before you go up steps'. Pulling a chair onto the landing, she made Ann climb onto the chair with the baby in her arms before letting her take him down the staircase.

A lady known as Mrs. Morgan the Toy Shop who lived on Twyn Hill, sold china, groceries and a special brand of tea costing two shillings a quarter which was an exorbitant price when tea was a few pence. But Ann's mother liked a good strong cup of tea and though it was expensive she was able to afford a quarter each week out of the money she made as a dressmaker. When I heard Ann talk about Mrs. Morgan the Toy shop, it brought back memories of my own mother, who not only was in service with the lady but spent the first few years of her marriage in the two upstairs rooms. When a small house in Baili Glas Court went vacant, Mrs. Morgan made sure it was let to my parents and when they moved out, she gave mother a beautiful Royal Albert twelve cup teaset which at present occupies the place of honour in my buffet sideboard.

Every year on the 1st of April, the lane owned by the Webster family of 'Ty Gwyn' house, was closed for one day to demonstrate it was not

60

a public footpath. This lane was not only a short cut to town but a quick way to the railway station so there was a continual stream of people up and down it throughout the day and most of the night.

On the morning of this special day, Ann and a number of her schoolmates were up at the crack of dawn to watch the barriers being erected by gardeners from 'Ty Gwyn'. Dangling their feet on the wall opposite, they wouldn't say a word as person after person made their last minute dash through the lane as usual in order to catch the valley train. They were stunned on finding the exit blocked as a good many of them didn't have the slightest idea of the alternative route.

As you can guess, the children were hysterical when they heard the whistle of the valley train fade in the distance leaving half its passengers behind.

'The air was blue with curses and unmentionable swear words as teachers and business men realised they had not only missed the train, but were now obliged to take the long way round plus wait a further hour for the next train to arrive', Ann wiped the tears from her eyes on recalling the incident.

The children were up to all sorts of tricks especially her best friend Lily Litchfield who made up large brown paper parcels filled with rolled up newspapers. When Lily spied someone the other end of the street, one of the famous parcels was thrown into the middle of the pavement where it was impossible to miss seeing it. Hiding in a doorway, the girls watched as the person bent quickly to pick the parcel up, popping it into a shopping bag. When the person had gone, they would be hysterical with laughter because inside the parcel Lily had written in big letters,

EVER BEEN HAD

A friend of her mothers called Mrs. Williams happened to be housekeeper to John Morgan the Ragged Sunday School and many times Ann accompanied her to his home in Thomas Street.

'Mr. Morgan was kind to poor children but tight as a chicken's bum to his housekeeper. For example, everything Mrs. Williams bought had to be written down for checking. If Mrs. Williams bought provisions in a different store the goods would sometimes be a penny or two extra which meant the housekeeping money wasn't sufficient to cover the cost of the goods. In which case the deficit had to be paid from Mrs. Williams own pocket!'

'His kitchen was loaded with sugar, tea, butter, biscuits, in fact everything his helpers needed to feed poor children. On the dressing table in his splendid bedroom, was a box of small brown packets each containing a three penny bit. Once I was lucky to find one of these

A classroom in Ann's day.

packets near his doorstep but as no-one came to claim it, I decided to keep it myself.'

When Ann's little sister Dolly was admitted to the Mardy Hospital with scarlet fever, the family used to stand outside the ward window and wave to her. Not even the parents were allowed inside the hospital in case of spreading the infection, so to keep the child happy they bought her a china doll which was handed to the nurse on duty.

Ann watched through the window as the doll was given to her little sister but instead of being pleased, Dolly threw her gift across the ward and the family saw it smash into pieces against the wall. Horrified they listened as Dolly screamed out;

'I don't want a stinking doll, I want to go home with Mammy'.

Another day, Ann was walking along Queen's Road after fetching her brother from school when a cow came charging towards them. Turning down the lane facing Thomastown Park they took a short cut into Union Street coming face to face with the cow. They ran like mad down the narrow steps with the cow behind them and pushing the door open of the first house they came to, hid in the passage till the cow had gone.

Ann cannot remember what the occasion was when dressed in a nightdress and clutching her rag doll, she was given a shilling for walking across the stage of the Old Drill Hall and having to walk back again.

'Next time you come to Victoria House I'll tell you more about what I used to do as a little girl', promised Ann, so one day soon I'm going to pay her another visit to listen to her happy memories.

Annie May Upham

Aaron Roberts
born 14th December, 1896

Aaron is one of the oldest residents to take part in my workshops and all his recollections are based on what it was like to work as an errand boy when he was just a lad.

At eight in the morning before going to school, he cleaned the outside windows, washed the tiled step and polished the brass plate of the grocer shop. Once school was over, Aaron picked up his bike fitted with a front basket to deliver the day's orders in fair or foul weather. Being small for his age, the lad of eleven found the special bike with the grocer's name plate fastened to the top bar, difficult to handle. Using his initiative he removed the plate allowing him to ride between the bar instead of over it. Heavy goods such as sacks of white or red potatoes costing five shillings or seven and six a hundred weight, had to be taken on a hand truck to all parts of the town.

Each Monday night after closing there were two 56lb chests of tea ready for Aaron to weigh into quarters and half pounds. Once the tea was weighed, the shop owner would flat wrap it personally, which was an art in itself, coming from years of experience. It would be 9 or 10 o'clock before both tea chests were empty and Aaron was dismissed.

'The smell of tea combined with continual bending gave me a blinding headache and I was glad to get home and crawl into bed.'

The rest of the week consisted of delivering orders, weighing up lentils, dried fruit, rice, peas etc. but when it came to sticky dates, Aaron was only too happy to oblige. The shelves needed refilling constantly also the brass weights were kept highly polished, and I'm sure you can guess by now who was held responsible for these time consuming jobs.

'On Saturday I worked a full day and as I grew older, the owner allowed me to serve behind the counter. But I was still expected to stay late after work to refill the shelves, clean the counter, the utensils, and the warehouse. Every cardboard box had to be flattened and tied ready for salvage collection because this was wartime and food being scarce was put on ration. Customers were issued with ration books and nothing could be bought without coupons. My job was to sort out the various coupons, count them then post the envelope to the Ministry of Food office. For all this work I received eight shillings weekly.'

The old grocers shop   *Courtesy: Merthyr Public Libraries*

Aaron left school when he was 14 years old to work full time at the same store for a further year delivering, serving behind the counter and learning how to flat wrap, pack loose butter into perfect squares, slice cheese and bacon by hand with a razor-sharp knife. The shop owner refused point blank to buy a bacon slicer because the speed of cutting took away the flavour of the bacon. Maybe there was a lot of truth in his words because they sold a tremendous amount of bacon for a small grocer shop. During his last year at the shop, Aaron's wages rose to 21/- (£1.05) but on asking for a further rise, he was refused and gave in his notice. For the following two years he worked on a milk round for a much better wage but not liking the job, left to join a National Multiple concern.

'Some of the things I witnessed could certainly not be tolerated in this day and age. Shop cats would piddle in sacks of rice, sugar, or any loose products left open overnight. Things were in short supply that we couldn't afford to waste anything, which resulted in scooping out the discoloured food stuff and weighing up what was unsoiled.'

'Another favourite deception was soaking stale beef sausages in water over the weekend. By Monday morning the water had taken the wrinkles and the red colour from the skins so they'd be sold as pork sausages. The funny part was that women used to come in and ask for the pork sausage as they tasted nicer.'

A similar trick was played with loose butter. Three tubs marked up with different prices were placed near the shop door where people were able to taste best, medium or cheaper quality butter. The normal method then was to scrape some butter on a sixpenny bit and decide which tasted the best. The dearest butter was inevitably chosen by the customer. When the tub of most expensive butter was empty, the second tub was moved into its place and the cheapest butter became the next best and so on.

'The funniest thing of all, was the fact, that lots of customers saw me replacing the empty tub with the so called second choice, but no-one seemed to twig what was going on'.

Exactly the same procedure took place with the bacon. All the slices were cut from the same pig, but again the price differed for various cuts.

'I never remember any complaints about the 'pork sausages', the bacon or the cheap butter tasting the same as the most expensive. They were hard but happy days which certainly haven't done me any harm. At ninety six I can look back to my youth with pride or knowledge that I never tried to dodge hard work.

The Angel Buildings in Lower High Street had a roller skating rink which was open morning and afternoon. Skating was free between 11 am and noon but it cost sixpence to hire skates. From 2.30 'til 5 pm, the charge was sixpence to skate plus another sixpence if you wanted skates. But Aaron liked going to the Electric Cinema because the programme lasted so long, and he was able to stay there until it closed. Except for two special films, Aaron found it difficult to remember how many features were shown, but 'The Sign of the Cross' and 'The Life of Lord Roberts V.C', remained etched on his memory.

Another event he hasn't forgotten was the funeral of Colonel David Rees Lewis V.C. All the shops including the grocers' where he worked closed early in order to watch what promised to be the biggest funeral Merthyr had ever seen. The afternoon was dark and chilly but before joining the huge crowds lining the streets from Brecon Road to Cefn Cemetery, Aaron went round to Penydarren Park where the Battalions and Bands were being marshalled by their officers for the procession. The grounds opposite were black with civilians being placed in order of merit by the funeral organisers.

Aaron decided the best view would be on a wall overlooking the burial plot so catching the last tramcar before all traffic was stopped, he slipped into the cemetery through a gap in the wall and found a good spot where he could watch in comfort.

The funeral procession being a mile long, took half an hour to pass along the streets, while muffled Parish Church bells pealed the whole time. Three mounted police rode at the head of the procession followed by the Firing Squad in the charge of Captain D. Cope Harris, the Battalion Band of 5th Welsh Regiment, the Band of the Breconshire Regiment and the Bugle Band of the 5th Welsh Regiment. Next came the Gun Carriage with military pall bearers marching on either side. Then came the Colonel's horse led by two orderlies Aaron noticed that the riding boots decorated with black and white rosettes were reversed as were the reins, straps and wallets.

The chief mourners followed on foot behind, the 5th Battalion Welsh Regiment, the Borough Police under Chief Officer Wilson, Boy Scouts led by Scout Master Tasker. The Ambulance Corps, with Clerks and Officers of the County Courts bringing up the rear.

Then came the mourning coaches, private carriages filled with just floral tributes, and carriages carrying important people like Seymour Berry, J.T. Harrap, William Raymond the Canal Wharf, Gay the Postmaster, Howfield the Confectioner and Flooks the Jeweller.

'There were loads more but those were the only people I knew because they were local'.

The Firing Squad lined up outside the cemetery while the

procession filed past and followed behind to the place of internment. It was dark when the Firing Squad presented arms and fired three volleys as a farewell salute at the graveside. The drums played a roll and the bugles wailed out the Last Post. Once outside the cemetery, the Battalions formed into columns and headed by Bands, marched all the way home.

'I wouldn't have missed it for the world and can honestly say I've never seen a funeral to beat it yet'.

Aaron is well cared for at Victoria House and enjoys being with many of his old friends now residents at the home.

Aaron Roberts

Margaret Thomas
born 17th May, 1903

Margaret was second oldest of five children, three girls and two boys. Some of her earliest memories dealt with household chores usually set aside for Friday night and Saturday morning.

Being a family of seven meant the cutlery which was constantly in use became tarnished quickly. Each Friday night her mother emptied the drawer of knives, forks, and spoons for Margaret to clean with brick manufactured by Rogers the Stone Works Caedraw Merthyr and bought at the Cooperative Store in Union Street.

'It was jolly hard work getting them clean and needed a lot of elbow grease for a little girl but as my brothers and sisters also had jobs to do, it wasn't so bad'.

The toilet was attached to the back wall of the house and it was Margaret's job on Saturday mornings to scrub the wooden seat until it

Milwards 'The Butchers'. Notice the pig and bull head.

was clean enough to eat food off. Because her little sister was nine and a half years younger, their father was obliged to make a smaller wooden circle to fit into the existing seat. Apparently the little girl on one occasion had almost frightened the family to death when she all but fell through the big hole and into the bucket underneath. Margaret remembers nursing the same little sister in a flannel shawl in what was commonly referred to as the Welsh way of nursing a baby.

A further memory was going twice a week with her friend Lizzie May to the bakehouse near the Antelope Arms on Dowlais Top, both girls would be carrying a tin of dough under each arm. Some of the tins had 'Hovis' stenciled on the bottom and when the loaves of bread were baked, the word Hovis was stamped underneath. For a small fee, the girls were willing to carry bread all the way to Dowlais Top for neighbours but were warned not to do it for strangers. Just before Christmas tin after tin of yeast cake was taken to the bakehouse but it was Margaret's father who took the goose to the bakehouse on Christmas morning while the children opened their gifts.

'It was lovely to go into Merthyr High Street just before Christmas and see the shop window decorated with holly and imitation snow but the butchers went one better by displaying bulls heads and pigs with oranges in their mouths. It was a sight never to be forgotten', said Margaret with a sigh.

One year she found a toy sweet shop complete with a counter, till, trays of mixed toffee and small glass jars full of sweets on the tiny shelves. Another year she had a drapery store with everything you'd find in a real draper's. There were small rolls of velvet, satin and brocade plus trimmings for curtains and lace for edging underwear. On her tenth birthday she had a rolled gold watch from her father and thought it was the finest watch in the world.

Beside being a hairdresser, Howells the Barber Shop, Dowlais, sold daily papers and Margaret loved to wait with the boys for the bundles of newspapers to be thrown out at Caeharris Station. What fun it was to watch the boys race each other across the platform in an effort to be the first away with their individual bundle!

The big Drapery Store near the gates of Guest Keen & Nettlefolds was owned by J.S. Davies and every New Year's morning children from all over the borough would queue up waiting for a new copper penny. After receiving a penny, each child held a hand out to be stamped in case he or she rejoined the queue hoping to get a second penny.

Their house had a back door but the lane it opened into was too narrow for the coal delivery cart to get through. This meant each load of coal was tipped outside the front door. Then it was all hands on deck with every member of the family assisting. Margaret's job was to spread old sacks the length of the passage into the sitting room and through to the back door. The others would be filling the buckets ready for her mother to carry and if any neighbours offered to help they'd be given a few buckets of coal as payment. The small was always left in a pile outside for whoever wished to collect it.

In order to save matches, the children made paper spills to put in a round tin kept on the mantlepiece and after the dead cinders were shovelled into the ash bucket, the inside of the oven, the wall of the grate and the stone hearth were whitened with stoning.

Margaret like to knit and found out from one of her friends that possibly the Scotch Wool Shop facing Woolworths gave patterns free of charge. Down she went to town and into the wool shop. Sure enough, the assistant after asking what ply wool she was using, handed Margaret a book of patterns to choose from. Sometimes she bought a skein or two of wool but more times than not, she just went in to look through the many books to get a free pattern.

'I remember my mother taking me to R.T. Jones during their Winter Sale and buying a single bed so I could sleep on my own. The bill came to 19s 6d including the bed frame, wire mattress, bed, bolster and pillow case, then my mother bought me a lovely nightdress trimmed with lace for 3s/6d'.

The Waterloo House issued their own £1 vouchers to purchase whatever was required from the store. You paid a shilling a week for twenty one weeks until the voucher was paid for, then another could be purchased. For the £1 the parcel would contain,

1 pair of blankets - 2 pillowcases - 1 bale of towels - 1 large teacloth - 1 pair flanelette sheets - 1 bowlster case - 6 tea towels.

All the girls wore liberty bodices those days, which after continuous boiling felt like a bodice of tight elastoplast across the chest. It was considered highly indecent for a young lady to go out without wearing both a vest and one of those dreadful restricting garments.

'Just suppose you were knocked down and admitted to hospital', my mother would say, 'and you weren't wearing a vest or liberty bodice, I'd die of shame'. I don't know what she'd say about the modern generation going about half naked.

Happy carefree days at Pont Sarn.

There was quite a bit of excitement when a neighbour was picked up by the police for breaking and entering Cohen the Outfitters lock up shop in Victoria Street. He stole goods to the value of £1 4s 6d. 3 shirts, one dozen pairs of lilse stockings, 6 bloomers, and a shawl. At the trial, the man said he was walking along the street when a stranger handed him a brown paper parcel. On opening it at home he found to his horror it contained the goods said to be stolen from Mr. Cohen. In summing up, the judge remarked icily;

'If you expect the court to believe that, you've got another thing coming'.

After being charged, the man was ordered to return the goods and pay five shillings. Because he was unemployed an arrangement was made to pay three pence weekly. His wife was so ashamed that not long afterwards they moved over the valley to Tafarnau Bach.

'A common practice then, to stop a fretful child from crying throughout the night, was to add a few drops of 'Jones' Red drops to the last feed. I found from experience they really worked miracles. But I often wonder now, what was in the drops to put a child out for hours and whether they were as harmless as the advert led one to believe'.

I enjoyed talking to Margaret about her memories and I am looking forward to visiting her again in the near future.

Margaret Thomas

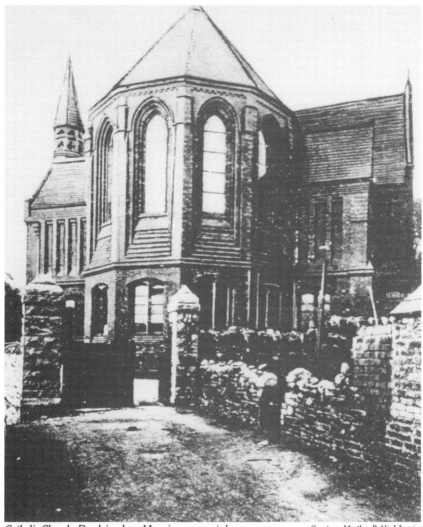

Catholic Church, Dowlais where Maggie was married.

Maggie Stephens
born 21st August, 1905

There were already three children from a previous marriage when Maggie's mother while visiting Ebbw Vale met Charles Alexander Thom, who was there on leave from his regiment, the South Wales Borderers. Her first husband went out to Pennsylvania and found work in the Pittsburgh steel works but was drowned in the Johnstown floods. Eventually a second marriage took place and a further five children brought the total to seven, owing to little Billy a child of the first union dying in infancy.

Being the youngest child, Maggie was spoilt silly by the others and not allowed to lift a finger to help when household chores were handed out because she was their 'Baby Sister'. This was all very well for a while but she didn't want to be pampered for the rest of her life by older brothers and sisters. As Maggie grew older she was determined to make a career for herself and because her brother was also extremely clever at school, her hopes were centred on an academic career for them both. Unfortunately, her mother wasn't interested in what was happening at school and never seemed to have the time to discuss their future.

The Sewing Class. *Courtesy: Merthyr Public Libraries*

'That's one thing I really regret, not being able to make Mammy understand the importance of being properly educated, though she worked hard to keep us well dressed and well fed, I don't think she gave my aspirations a second thought. I can understand her thinking that marriage was all a girl was cut out for but it was different for my brother as one day he'd have a family to support and education meant a better way of life. I often think to myself how different things are today, when parents are only too anxious to sit down with their children and listen to their plans for the future. I only wish my brother and I could have done just that'.

Maggie recalls having her hair wound into rag strips each night before going to bed and in the morning when her mother unwound the rags, she'd have six lovely ringlets. Her older sister Hannah, had been sent by the catholic priest to learn her trade with an excellent seamstress called Miss Primavasey. During her training, Hannah made gorgeous dressses and pinafores for her little sister who was always the best dressed child in the class.

R.T. Jones & Co. High Street, Merthyr used to have a Winter sale each year during which they sold clothes, bedding, household goods, and furniture at reduced prices. It was at one of these sales that Maggie's mother treated herself to a tailor made costume for one guinea, a skirt for two shillings and eleven pence and a beaver fur set for each of the younger girls at one shilling and halfpenny a set.

Maggie was ready to go to school one morning when a neighbour mentioned that Big Dan was being taken to the cells in Market Square Police Station about ten o'clock. She ran all the way from Georgetown to get there before the Black Maria arrived. Market Square was crowded with people all eager to see the murderer but being small Maggie pushed hersef to the front of the crowd. It appeared that Big Dan had killed his wife in a fit of temper but some women standing near Maggie said his wife was no good and he'd been driven to murder. When the Black Maria eventually turned up, a policeman stood right in front of the little girl so she couldn't see a thing but it didn't matter because as Big Dan was covered with a blanket no-one else saw him either.

Maggie was another of the hundreds of children flocking on New Year's Day to receive one of J.S. Davies new pennies straight from the mint. There were so many children that it took six policemen to keep the streets clear.

'It was ridiculous when I think of it now. It cost me a penny on the tram to pick up another penny to pay for the tram ride back. If Mr. Davies had already emptied his bag, I not only forfeited my penny but was obliged to walk from Dowlais to Georgetown.

When her best friend became parlour maid at Pentrebach House, Maggie also wanted to try her hand at service. One sister was already working for Mr. Richards the architect in private service and was treated very well so Maggie joined the staff at Pentrebach House as a general maid. She stuck it out for two months. The house belonged to Mr. Sankey the owner of Plymouth Colliery but it was occupied by Mr. Thomas, one of his managers. He expected Maggie to look after the

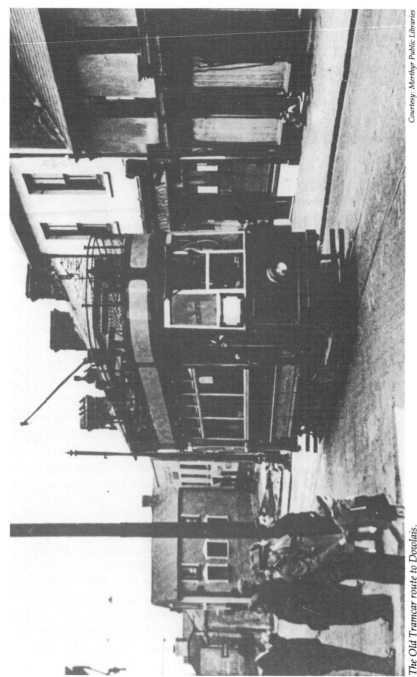

The Old Tramcar route to Dowlais.

78

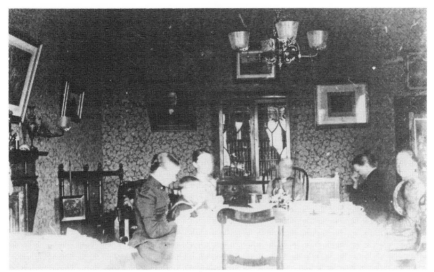

The Dining Room at Pentrebach House, Merthyr.

children as well as the general cleaning so she packed the job in. Next, she had a job delivering bread round the doors for Mr. Morris the Bakehouse, Merthyr Road, Penydarren. The salary was half a crown weekly and free bread but it was hard work specially on weekends when the bakehouse tables had to be cleaned. The girls weren't allowed to use water but had to clean the sticky surfaces with flour and cloths full of fat. This job lasted for the best part of a year before Maggie got fed up and gave in her notice.

While at the bakehouse one of the bakers told her how to make a dessert called 'Sybil's Pudding', from a packet of Cakeoma (the quick mix of the day) plus the following ingredients;

6ozs butter or dripping - 2 eggs - milk as required - 1 desert spoon of brandy - small jar preserved ginger - pinch of salt

Method

Empty Cakeoma into bowl, rub in ingredients. Add milk, mix into a thick batter. Boil in a greased basin for three hours. Serve with sauce.

Sauce

Half pint milk, quarter pint water, 1 tablespoon flour, 1 tablespoon sugar, wineglass brandy or sherry. Mix and bring to boil.

Reading the Merthyr Express one night she noticed an interesting advert inviting shop assistants and other members of the public to join a painting class. Inquiries were to be made at a shop in Glebeland Street but after learning the lessons were for two hours and expensive, Maggie changed her mind and went instead to see 'The Sleeping Beauty', at the Electric Theatre. The nice thing about going to see a film at the Electric was the fact that whatever time you went in you'd be able to see the picture. By going early you'd see the main feature at least twice.

Maggie never missed the annual pantomine at the Theatre Royal but the one she enjoyed most was 'Babes in the Wood', but as she grew older her choice fell to the wonderful stage plays like, 'The King's Romance', 'The Sport of Kings', or plays by George Bernard Shaw which were performed nightly at the Theatre Royal.

Advertisements citing miraculous cures by some medicine or ointment held a fascination for Maggie the teenager. One advert in the Merthyr Express of about 1912 still brings tears to the eyes. Beneath the picture of a robust little girl were the following words.

This CHILD was RESCUED from a WASTING DEBILITY
by taking DR. WILLIAMS PINK PILLS

Another in the same paper read as follows;

A WHOLE FAMILY WAS CURED FROM ECZEMA BY APPLYING ZAM-BUK.

Maggie got married at eighteen and settled down to rear a family of her own.

In 1990 she became a resident at Victoria House and enjoys being able to associate with friendly people of her own generation.

Maggie Stephens

Jim Evans
born 10th April, 1911

Jim was the youngest of eight children and is fortunate enough to have two birthdays. When he was born if a child wasn't registered within three weeks of birth the date appearing on the birth certificate would be the day it was issued which in this case was 30th April, 1911.

The other week Jim heard a programme on the television about a case similar to his own. A Cardiff lady was enjoying her ninety fifth birthday at a special party given by her family when a telegram was handed to her. It was from Queen Elizabeth wishing the old lady, many happy returns of the day on reaching a hundred years of age. An investigation was carried out at the Registration Office of Births & Deaths and it appears that five years had passed before someone registered the child. As a result the date on the certificate was the day of issue not the date of birth.

Courtesy: Merthyr Public Libraries

J.S. Davies & Co., Dowlais.

Jim has many interesting memories to relate including some already told by other residents of Dowlais. For example, he also went to collect a shiny new penny from J.S. Davies on New Year's Day but was never lucky enough to dodge the indelible stamp that refused to wash off until it was too late to claim another penny.

The Oddfellows Hall, Dowlais was used for a variety of entertainment and when films became the in thing, an electric motor was installed for this very purpose. One night the picture went off in the middle of a film and Jim's father in trying to fix the motor, managed to get his hand twisted in the machinery. As a result of the accident, Jim's father contracted lockjaw and died in a very short time.

Though he was only seven, Jim remembers as clear as yesterday his Mam dressed from head to toe in black and the coffin bearers wearing bowler hats and frock tail coats.

On New Year's Day, The Oddfellows Hall and Victoria Cinema let children in to see the film free of charge. With a new penny in his pocket, Jim would join the queue outside one of the cinemas, picking up a free bag of sweets inside. Having seen the one show through he'd join the other line of children outside the other cinema remaining there till closing.

The first film Jim saw at The Victoria Cinema was Charlie Chaplin in 'The Gold Rush', which today is acclaimed as a classic from the silent screen. But what really had him pinned to the seat and biting his nails was the famous episode in one of Pearl White's films where the bandits tied her to the rail road track. As the train came thundering towards her, the following words would flash across the screen,

'To be continued next week'

But as one would expect, she was rescued in the nick of time by a dare devil hero.

The first Chinese Laundry in Wales was situated at the bottom of Brecon Road, Dowlais and it was here that Jim took his brothers' collars to be washed, stiffened and ironed for the costly sum of sixpennies each. Jim also recalls Reg Lee who wrote 'The Town that Died', being born in Horse Street.

Each Tuesday evening the Band of Hope was held at Caersalem Chapel with a deacon called Dafydd Mylor conducting the singing. On his way to the Band of Hope, Dafydd Mylor would call at every public house on route and call down damnation on all those gathered there. Pushing the pub door wide open he'd stand where everyone could see him and preach hellfire and brimstone.

'Before the devil brought you to this den of iniquity, your souls were pure and whiter than snow, now they are ugly black from drinking. When you finally arrive at the pearly gates they'll be barred against sinners and your lot will be in the fiery furnace that burns forever.'

Such strong words induced many to join the Band of Hope but others made mock of Dafydd telling him to go away and mind his own business.

Jim lived above the Duke Public House. As it was illegal to drink on Sunday, the police kept a watchful eye on the Duke, but the locals were one ahead of the law. After getting a skinful, they went through a door leading into an alley at the back of the pub, over the wall and through the passage door used by Jim's family leading out onto the main road. Of course, anyone seeing the offenders assumed they'd been visiting the Jones Family living above the premises.

When times were bad, unemployed men spent most of their time searching for coal in the Patches to be sold at one shilling and threepence a bag. There were always queues of people outside 'Isgoed' house where clothes and shoes were given out to needy families and Jim remembers one of their neighbours receiving £1 2s 6d to keep a family of eight in food and clothing.

The Merthyr Express was always loaded with remedies to cure ailments of every description such as Deakins Lung Healer guaranteed to cure any chest complaint in record time. Another miraculous cure was a unique remedy from J.E. George for Piles and

Gravel. Unfortunately the miners continued to spit up coal dust, and passed gravel without let-up but hope springs eternal so they carried on taking the tablets.

Below the Parish Church, Merthyr were the Turkish Baths and it was grand to lie in the stream watching the dirt pour out from the body and collect on top of your skin. One would feel stones lighter on coming out of the baths but the nicest thing of all was to feel really clean. Tuesday was Ladies Only and on that day there'd be a nurse in attendance because the weaker sex were prone to fainting off in the tremendous heat.

Old Turkish Baths, Lower High Street, Merthyr. *Courtesy: Merthyr Public Libraries*

'My mother was very critical about the length of ladies' clothes. I suppose today she'd be considered narrow minded, but I remember clearly listening to her gossiping with our neighbour about the woman living opposite. It seems the person under discussion had worn a new dress to chapel which was shorter than it should have been'.

'Fancy showing her face in chapel wearing clothes above her ankles, I've never seen anything so vulgar or disgusting', my mother raved on and on about young hussies bent on giving our street a bad name.

'I don't think I ever tasted coffee, my mother always gave us either Rowntree's or Bournville Cocoa with our meals and Horlicks Malted Milk at bedtime. Whenever I caught the tram to town, I made a beeline

HOWFIELD

AND **SON,**

Telephone No. 0187.

Telegrams :
"Howfield, Merthyr."

WHOLESALE & MANUFACTURING

CONFECTIONERS,

MERTHYR TYDFIL.

S PECIAL CARE and attention is de-
voted to the manufacture of Cake of
every description, by the latest and
most up-to-date methods. The purest
and most wholesome ingredients only are
used, and patrons may rely upon obtain-
ing the best possible value for money.

SWEETS of every description and at all prices.

One of the largest stocks in Wales to select from.

for Howfield's shop to buy 2 ozs of their special caramels which cost 3½ pennies a quarter and a quarter of cream toffees for my mother costing 5 pennies. Everyone wants to diet these days but we ate tons of fat ham, bacon, bread and dripping without growing fat. Beside surviving to a ripe old age, I'm lucky enough to have all my marbles so dripping didn't do me any harm'.

Jim couldn't spare any more time to chat, he was off on his rounds to meet some old mates.

Jim Evans

Eileen Edwards
born 10th October, 1903

Eileen was the middle child in a family of three and one of her earliest recollections is of being allowed to stay up late one night when as a rule she was made to go to bed very early. Another strange occurrence was the arrival of her grandmother after dark, so putting two and two together, the child knew something was up. The following morning Eileen was left in bed until her grandma came into the bedroom and after kissing her said,

'Come and see your new baby brother'.

It appears the family were afraid that she would be jealous of the baby but their fears proved groundless as Eileen idolised little Cyril to such an extent that her mother warned,

'Remember this Eileen, you mustn't love anyone more than you love God'.

Emrys Morgan worked in the offices of Guest Keen & Nettlefolds as a staff accountant which was a good position with a reasonable salary. During the visit of King George and Queen Mary to Dowlais, a special stand was erected for the managers and staff of Guest Keen Works so

Courtesy: Merthyr Public Libraries

that they should have a good view of the Royal party. Eileen was proud as a peacock to see both her parents on the special elevated platform, as she pointed them out to her schoolmates.

Courtesy: Merthyr Public Libraries

'We'd waited hours to see the King and Queen but the car whizzed passed us and all I saw was a gloved hand. It was nothing but a waste of time'.

When Alfred W. Houlson the secretary of G.K.N. Ltd. died of pneumonia, both her parents were invited to the funeral. Being a J.P. the deceased was well known and respected throughout the Borough so as one would expect most of Merthyr's dignitaries walked behind an impressive glass hearse drawn by a pair of black draped horses. The streets were crowded with spectators as the cortege moved slowly towards the cemetery and Eileen waited excitedly for the cab carrying her parents to pass by.

Owing to Emrys Morgan's good job, the family could afford to spend their annual holiday at the seaside town of Mumbles. Only on two occasions can Eileen recall going elsewhere, the exceptions being one visit to Weston another to Aberystwyth.

Days before the holiday, their mother would be busy washing and ironing summer frocks, shirts and changes ready for packing. On Friday after school the children would lean over the half open kitchen window and watch their mother packing their bathing suits, buckets and spades into a big brown tin trunk.

The horse and cab arrived early on Saturday morning and once the cabby loaded the trunk and portmantoes, they'd be on their way to the Mumbles. Eileen was now nine and having saved her pocket money, gave three year old Cyril, two pennies for himself. One afternoon, the family were on their way to the pier when Cyril ran off on his own. He returned clutching an ice cream cone purchased with the two pennies. Their parents were horrified and looked around to see if anyone they knew had seen what Cyril had done.

'It's a sin to buy ice cream on the sabbath', screamed his mother, 'put it in the nearest bin quickly before the minister hears of it'.

Despite little Cyril's cries and pleas the ice cream cone was thrown into the first bin they saw.

Because he was the eldest of the family, Arthur felt dutybound to protect his younger sister but unfortunately, Eileen didn't want anyone keeping an eye on her movements particularly, an over protective brother. This caused constant skirmishes between them until Arthur shouted out in temper,

'Can't you see I'm looking after your welfare, which you've been doing to our Cyril since he was born', so they smoked the pipe of peace.

Eileen's mother had a beautiful trained voice and after chapel on Sunday the family would gather around the piano in the middle room

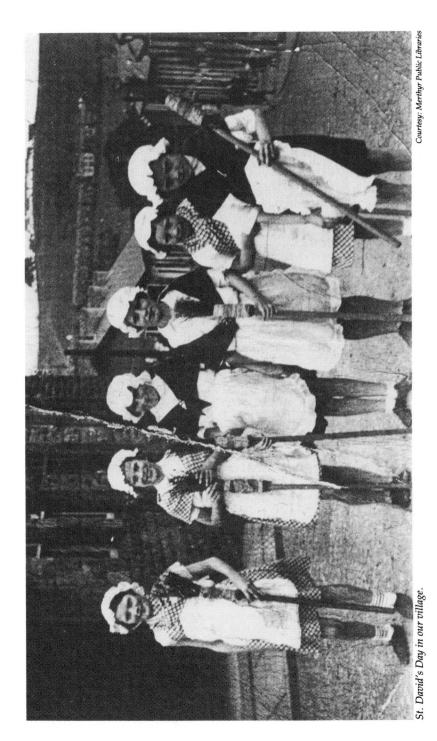

St. David's Day in our village.

91

to sing hymns. Other nights their mother would invite friends to a musical evening and entertain them by singing arias and the children's favourite songs. One of her mother's special gifts was the ability to impersonate a very well known Italian boy soprano, which went down a treat during musical evenings.

'My favourite was 'Just a Song at Twilight', because no one sang it the way Mama used to', said Eileen, smiling sadly as she recalled those long gone evenings around the piano.

The family attended Eisteddfodau as far distant as Abergavenny or Mountain Ash on Easter Monday. Light operettas were very popular in the valleys and when Joseph Parry's opera 'Bodwen', was performed in the Kirkhouse Hall, Eileen's mother sang in the chorus. Hope Church Merthyr held organ recitals with supporting artists and Eileen recalls her father reserving seats for all the family at a cost of three shillings each to hear Master Charles W. Langley, the famous boy soprano sing at one of the recital concerts.

'When one compares old prices with the escalating costs of today, they seem absurd. I remember my father buying a satin wardrobe bedroom suite, complete with bed frame spring and mattress, for £6.12.6 round about 1911 or 1912 during a Winter sale at R.T. Jones & Co. High Street, Merthyr. Most people bought oilcloth or linoleum to cover their floors and staircases but father bought 18 inch wide carpet for our stairs and I remember mother shouting angrily at Cyril.'

'That carpet cost three and six a yard, so stop wearing it out by running up and down the staircase'.

One day, a gasman came to the house to install a penny slot meter. When the gas went out later that evening, Eileen asked her father for a second penny.

'Whatever are you doing with the gas', demanded her father, 'I've already put one penny in the meter this morning. Do you think I'm made of money?'

After a fire which could have turned out to be the biggest blaze Merthyr had ever seen, was expertly contained, Southey & Sons 'Express' office inserted a giant advert in the Merthyr Express which brought the people flocking to their shop in Glebeland Street.

The advert read as follows;

Great Salvage Sale
Everything Must Go
PRICES ROCK BOTTOM

Eileen took Cyril in the pram to see what her pocket money could buy but there was nothing left worth having when she eventually got inside.

That was a long time ago. Now Eileen is happily settled in Victoria House, Dowlais, but as she remarked to me,

'I enjoy talking about the old days, especially when someone is really interested'.

Eileen hasn't been a resident for very long at Victoria House but she is happy and very contented to be among loving companions and a caring staff.

Eileen Edwards

Workshop in progress at Victoria House.

Officer Mrs. Heather Paul enjoying the interchange of recollections.

Staff and workshop group.

Waiting to start a workshop session.

Myself and four of my star participants.

Staff joining in photograph at close of session.

Gurnos Home,
Gurnos Estate, Merthyr

Courtesy: Meirion Davies

Courtesy: Val Evans

Maggie May Jones
born 22nd December, 1904

Maggie May is one of seven children brought up in the Rhymney Valley. As a very small child she suffered from lack of energy and being so poorly was unable to attend school. The doctor diagnosed T.B. but there was no clinic, hospital or sanitorium nearby where Maggie May could be sent for treatment. It was essential that the child was kept away from other children so her mother agreed to send the little girl to live with her grandma.

The old lady was a semi-invalid and though able to move around the house, was unable to go outside. The situation would have presented a major problem with Maggie May also being confined to the house until the doctor saw fit to state otherwise.

'My Auntie May worked for a newsagent in Rhymney and being a spinster still lived at home with Grandma. This meant she could buy whatever we needed to eat from the grocer shop next door to where she worked.'

There were no shops where they lived in Pontlottyn, so Maggie May's auntie used to bring packets containing five Cinderella cigarettes from the newsagent's, to sell to friends and neighbours.

'You couldn't buy anything worth having in the small Rhymney shops so Auntie May went to Cardiff on her day off every month, to buy powder, face cream and perfumed soaps. I remember the little books where every page was saturated with a different shade of powder. After choosing the right shade to match whatever she was wearing, my aunt would remove the page and rub it into her skin while the powder lasted. She bought my clothes at Seccombes and paid for them herself. Unlike my sisters, I didn't have to wear garments passed down from one to the other. I suppose I was quite spoilt by Grandma and Auntie May for ten happy years without being aware of the fact.'

Maggie May's aunt, insisted they both slept in the same bed in case her niece felt unwell during the night. This solved a problem that had worried the little girl since she knew she had to move to Pontlottyn. At home, the girls had to share beds and the thought of being alone in a room of her own, owing to her hating the dark, had been worrying the little girl. Grandma on the other hand slept in a beautiful French four poster bed, and although she gave her granddaughter carte-blanche in most instances. When Maggie May asked if she could join her Grandma in the four poster bed, she was refused point blank.

Grandma, I love you.

As already mentioned, Maggie May was not allowed out of the house, so she couldn't attend school. Her day was split up between amusing herself and resting when she felt tired, or maybe watching her Grandma concoct herbal mixtures and smelly ointments. The house was seldom free from individuals seeking advice for ailments that doctors failed to cure.

'Why can't you cure me then, Grandma?', asked Maggie May one day.

'Because there's nothing seriously wrong with you except for a bit of anaemia which you'll soon grow out of.'

'But the doctor said I'd never be well enough to play like other girls my age', persisted Maggie May now almost 10 years of age.

'We'll wait and see', the old lady would reply.

A young mother with a month old baby, living next door, found she had a gathered breast which was very painful. The local doctor was called in but his treatment proved unsuccessful and instead of getting better, the breast became badly infected.

'I'll have to admit you to Abergavenny Hospital as soon as there's a bed available', said the doctor looking very worried.

'Polly's crying blue murder because she has to go to hospital, Grandma, and she's afraid she'll die', said Maggie May excitedly.

'Ask her into the kitchen and fetch a shawl from upstairs'.

Polly sat in the big wooden armchair watching the old lady prepare one of her magical cures. First she put a lump of lard to heat in an iron frying pan. When the fat melted, flour was stirred in to form a stiff paste and the lot was spread onto a clean piece of cloth with a hole cut out for the nipple. The mother gave an agonising scream as the poultice was applied and passed out completely.

'Cover her with the shawl, she'll come round soon', said Grandma, not in the least perturbed at seeing Polly slumped in a heap.'

Sure enough, Polly recovered in a few minutes, declaring she felt ten times better already, and a hundred times better by the time she downed a hot cup of tea half filled with gin. Within a couple of days, the gathering had cleared up, to the utter amazement of the local doctor.

'Another day, an old gentleman who couldn't lift his head because of a massive carbuncle on his neck, came to Grandma for help.'

Maggie May was sent to the garden for some chickweed, which was washed dried, chopped up fine, mixed with lard and placed on the man's neck. Each day he came to have the dressing changed and at the end of the week the old lady pulled the carbunkle out, roots and all.

'Grandma made gallons of ginger ale which I helped bottle ready for the customers when they called. One neighbour who came regularly, said she was having trouble getting to sleep, and could Grandma suggest something to take. I was sent to the brewery for a penny bag of hops.'

'Place a handful of these under your pillow every night, Bertha', were Grandma's instructions to our neighbour, 'and you'll sleep like a top'.

The remedy worked and before long the brewery was inundated

with people wanting hops. I was fascinated to learn, that only a few days before I spoke with Maggie May, she'd read in a magazine, about a Northampton firm who were about to manufacture hop filled pillows for people suffering from acute insomnia. Which goes to prove that old fashioned remedies are not to be laughed at.

'Instead of 'using the knife', in the operating theatre, many serious complaints were cured in people's own kitchen's,' said Maggie May, 'Let's take tonsillitis for example. To us it was simply a 'Sore Throat', cured by closing your eyes, opening your mouth wide, and blowing in 3d worth of sulphur. Next, the throat was smeared with goose grease and bound with red flannel for a couple of days. Grandma cured crippling attacks of stomach ache by taking down a bunch of the dried wormwood hanging from one of the kitchen beams, soaking it in hot water and drinking the mixture when cool.'

For ten happy years, Maggie May lived with her relatives without any problems arising. Suddenly, the old lady died, and everything changed.

Neighbours scrubbing their doorsteps. *Courtesy: Merthyr Public Libraries*

'What's Maggie May going to do, with her aunt out working all day?', was the big question. 'If she didn't have T.B. we'd have her home', said her mother, 'but we have six other children to consider, and it wouldn't be fair on them.'

'Grandma said I had nothing more that a bit of anaemia which has gone completely', retorted Maggie May angrily.

After much discussion, Maggie May was taken for a second opinion. A new x-ray, proved her grandmother correct. The specialist confirmed that she had had a form of anaemia, but good packing and rest had done the trick. So Maggie May went home to a different way of life.

Her parents were good-living Christians who never sat down to eat until a blessing had been asked, and each night at bedtime their father would sit and listen to their prayers. When prayers were over he used to add;

'And God bless the sailors who bring our food home across rough seas'.

Then he'd put out the oil lamp.

Instead of being left alone to her own devices, Maggie May was given work to do like carrying tins of bread to the bakehouse, scrubbing dirty slate steps, filling the lamps with smelly paraffin, or cleaning the brasses each Friday night. Life was hard and hateful but the worse thing of all was wearing cast-off-clothing, when her own pretty dresses wore out.

Being something of an extrovert, she recited popular poems like 'The Orphan Boy's Tale', and 'Somebody's Mother', in chapels, churches and Penny Readings.

'My services were free of charge with the occasional Fry's coconut bar slipped into my pocket by an appreciative listener'.

Later, Maggie May branched out into Gilbert and Sullivan's operettas. Her favourites were 'Pirates of Penzance', 'The Gondoliers', and 'The Yeoman of the Guard'. So all in all there weren't many dull moments in her life.

Her parents' house was neat and clean with furniture polished enough to see your face in it. The solid mahogany chest of drawers in the parlour had been in the family for many years and Maggie May was fascinated by a mahogany framed swing mirror standing on the top. Underneath the mirror was a secret drawer, to keep jewellery or important documents. Beside the mirror, there were a pair of black and white china dogs and a ruby carousel with crystal jinglers hanging all the way around.

At 16 years of age Maggie May decided it was time to earn some money. From 9am to 5pm, she cleaned and washed for anyone willing to pay 2/6 a day.

'Now the shoe is on the other foot and everything is done for me by the staff. But it's nice to relax after years of hard work and look back on the way life used to be', said Maggie May smiling happily.

Maggie May Jones

The Hughes family.

Gwladys Muriel Roberts
born 13th October, 1908

'I can't tell you about myself until I explain a little about Dad, who involved me from an early age in his business. As a result, I knew all there was to know about horses and the work of a smithy'.

Penydarren residents still talk affectionately about 'Hughes the Blacksmith', who shod horses, cured their ailments, extracted their teeth and performed delicate operations when the need arose. His business which spanned fifty years was forced to move forward when automation took over the service once carried out by the horse and cart. Being a man of clear perception, William Morgan Hughes turned his sights to welding railings, gates, ornamental iron work and shoeing the occasional horse.

It all started on the train taking Mr. Hughes and his bride on their honeymoon to Llanstephan. Mr. Seymour Berry, later known as Lord Buckland happened to be going to the same seaside resort and during the journey the two men started up a conversation.

'Where are you employed?', inquired Seymour Berry.

Mr. Hughes replied, 'I worked in a level but conditions went from bad to worse. There wasn't a night when I didn't arrive home drenched to the skin, so I decided to quit'.

'What will you do now, Mr. Hughes?'

'Start my own business as a blacksmith, if I can raise the money'.

'And where will your premises be?' asked Mr. Seymour Berry.

'In the shed behind my house', was the reply.

'If you manage to raise the capital, I can put a great deal of business your way and that's a promise'.

Seymour Berry talked about his place in Bwlch, Brecon, where he stabled his hunting horses. Before parting at Llanstephan a verbal agreement was made between them to the effect, that all shoeing for Mr. Seymour Berry would be done by William Morgan Hughes, if things turned out as planned. Shortly after their discussion, news arrived that Mr. Hughes had started up a blacksmith business, in the shed at the rear of his house. In no time at all, 'Hughes the Blacksmith', was known near and far, not only for shoeing horses but treating their ailments successfully.

Fetching bread from the bakehouse.   *Courtesy: Merthyr Public Libraries*

Four of the eleven children born to Mrs. Hughes died in infancy. Then came Ceinwen, Brynley, Idris, Phyllis, Gwladys and following a gap of thirteen years, Winnie and Handel were born. A specialist discovered that poor little Handel had no less than five holes in his heart. There was no known surgery as such to correct his serious condition, so when Handel survived to manhood, it was nothing short of a miracle.

Brynley and Gwladys were the two chosen to assist their father when a set of shoes needed to be replaced, or a bad tooth extracted from a very nervous horse. They had no electricity in the shed, so Gwladys held the lamp while Brynley and his brother hung on like grim death to the horse. While performing any kind of operation on a sick animal, the startling effect brought about by their father's voice, was truly uncanny.

'Dad always spoke to the horse in Welsh. It is hard to believe but I knew the horse understood every word', said Gwladys, 'because once Dad began to speak, the animal calmed down and let him carry on doing whatever he had to do.'

There was always a horse waiting to be shod, or things needing to be done in the house, thus making it impossible for Gwladys to play after school with her friends. One day a close friend of the family mentioned in passing, that a little girl should be outside playing in the fresh air, instead of always indoors.

'Hard work never killed anyone', retorted Mrs. Hughes.

'It may not kill', was the quick reply, 'but it certainly leaves its mark.'

'When I think back', said Gwladys, 'Brynley and I were nothing but slaves. Mam said that lazy housewives, instead of making their own bread, bought it ready baked, but I often wished we could afford to buy shop bread. Every morning Mam filled a big basket with loaves and currant cakes ready for baking. As you can guess, it was Brynley and I who struggled up the hill to the bakehouse before going to school. Each afternoon when school was over, I changed into old clothes, made a flask of tea and joined Dad in the shed. It was work, work, and more work.'

Whenever their father was shoeing, Brynley worked the bellows, while his sister standing on two boxes, filed the shoe until it fitted snuggly on the hoof. The file was pushed in one direction, always to the right, so when the iron was removed from the vice it shone like silver.

One day Mr. Hughes received a message from Seymour Berry saying there was something so seriously wrong with Sergeant, his favourite hunter, that he'd been advised to have the horse shot. In reply, the blacksmith requested the hunter be brought to Merthyr in case there was something he could do to cure him. Early the following morning just as the children were preparing for school, a huntsman arrived with Sergeant.

'Don't let Dad see us' Brynley said, 'or he'll want us to help'.

Quiet as mice, they crept across the pebbled alley on tiptoe, but not quietly enough for their father's paper thin ears.

'I need you both to help me this morning', he shouted from the shed.

Shrugging their shoulders in defeat, the children made their way to the shed. The huntsman was trying to keep Sergeant calm while a furious Mrs. Hughes read the riot act to her husband for having the poor horse travel all the way from Bwlch.

'If he dies, Wil, you won't hear the end of this, your business will be ruined', she was mad with temper.

'They were going to shoot him anyway', retaliated her husband. 'Shut up woman, and look to your own work while I see to mine'.

Turning to the children he ordered them to run as fast as they could to Jenkins the Chemist in Merthyr for as many calico bandages as they could carry.

The huntsman retured to Bwlch with the following message.

'Don't worry Seymour, I know what's wrong with Sergeant, just give me a few days'.

Mr. Hughes stayed up two nights with the horse and on the third morning as Gwladys and Brynley were leaving for school, they heard him shout,

'I want you both up here at once to see something special'.

The shed was swimming with water and they could see Sergeant in the far corner.

'Stay outside and watch'.

Their father held the razorsharp knife he used for operations in his hand while he spoke softly in Welsh to Sergeant.

'Come to me, boy'. The horse moved slowly from the corner and laid his head on their father's shoulder.

'Have you ever seen anything like that before?'

The children shook their heads.

'I wish I had a camera, Dad', said Brynley starting to cry.

'Are you going to kill him?', asked Gwladys, sick with fright.

'Kill him?', replied her father 'I've just cured him, the water you see poured from Sergeant's brain as the pressure troubling him was released'.

'Can't you see how thankful the poor beggar is'.

When they got to school, Miss Price the head mistress caned Gwladys without letting the child explain her reason for being late. Brynley fared even worse.

'Where have you been, boy?', demanded his teacher.

Brynley described in detail what had taken place in the shed.

'You're a liar, boy'. Picking up the phone he asked for Mr. Hughes.

'What's this fairy tale Brynley has made up to save having the cane?'

'No fairy tale, Mr. Davies but the truth', was the reply.

'Bullwash', Mr. Davies retorted.

'My children don't lie. I'll expect you at my premises before the horse goes back to Bwlch. Either you apologise or the matter will be taken up with the School Governors.'

Mr. Davies full of apologies, arrived at the forge within the hour.

On another occasion a horse named Simon was brought in to have a tooth extracted and Gwladys was summoned to hold a pole attached to the bridle in order to keep the horse's mouth open.

The Blacksmith's Forge   *Courtesy: Merthyr Public Libraries*

'Gwladys, you are shaking, girl. Simon will kick.'

'No Dad, I'm holding the pole steady, honest I am'.

William Hughes kept talking to the horse in Welsh until the three inch tooth was drawn and thrown into the furnace while Gwladys tipped salt into a bucket of water.

'Put your head in this bucket, my lad, rinse the blood from your mouth'.

The horse ducked his head at once into the salt water, and at the next command, shook his head back and fro in a second bucket of clear water.

'You're all right now, boyo', her father kept smoothing Simon's forelock.

The cost of shoeing back there was 12/6 for a cart horse or 6/6 for a pony.

As business improved, there were bills to be written and delivered on foot to clients as far away as Pontsticill and as usual it fell to our Gwladys to execute both jobs. The procedure never varied. First calls were to clients in Penydarren, from there to Penywern, Pengarnddu, Pant and into Pontsticill. Occasionally, the young girl would cadge a lift on a milk or bread cart but most times it meant hours of walking along rough lanes. When the bill was handed to a certain grocer living in Penywern, instead of money, he'd give the girl a bag of groceries, in spite of Gwladys insisting she couldn't go home without money. The bag of groceries got heavier with every step as Gwladys made for the farm at Pontsticill. The old farmer forever pleading poverty, would cut a chunk off some fat bacon with a single streak of lean through the middle.

'Tell your father I'm a bit short this week, take this bacon on account.'

It was no use arguing with him. Picking up the groceries and the lump of fat bacon, Gwladys began the long trek home to Penydarren.

Together, the family spoke in their native tongue which accounted for Gwladys at eighteen, speaking a mixture of two languages. This proved an embarrassment when she joined an Amateur Dramatic Society because the other members being pupils of Merthyr Intermediate School, had a good grounding of the King's English.

Calling the young girl aside, after a rehearsal, the stage manager said,

'Though your acting is satisfactory, I doubt whether broken English will go down well with the audience, but because it's our last play for the season, we'll give it a try'.

In fact, the audience loved her quaint mixture of Welsh and English and Gwladys was an overnight success, receiving thunderous applause at each performance. With the exception of Gwladys, the four other children on the family photograph left home to train for a profession.

Brynley became an Agricultural Blacksmith, Ceinwen went to a teachers training college at Dudley, Phyllis became a Matron in Bargoed Hospital and Idris ended up as a Registered Shoeing Smith.

'I remember Ceinwen applying for a full time post when she was employed as a side teacher. When Dad asked a councillor the reason for her being turned down time after time, he received the following answer.

'Your daughter hasn't a hope in hell of landing a job in Merthyr when your vote goes to the conservatives'.

Ceinwen eventually took a post in England and rose to Head Mistress.

Despite coming close to death in 1991, when a flash flood swept through Horeb Court Pentdarren and having to face the heartbreak of losing three of her family recently in an horrific fire. Gwladys at 85 years of age is one of the most interesting and informative people I have had in my workshops.

Gwladys Muriel Roberts

Stan Daniels
born 20th November, 1897

This was my first and only experience of a married couple both over ninety years of age who were able to join in my Workshop and talk about village life in Warminster, near Salisbury Plains. Both husband and wife were from the same village. As children, Stan and Lena attended the one and only village school but never had anything to do with each other. Lena happened to be friendly with Stan's sisters so she saw their older brother on various occasions but never took much notice of her.

Stan had five brothers, seven sisters and an invalid mother suffering from dropsy. They lived in a small thatched cottage on the Roundway Estate where his father like most other villagers, worked for Lord Roundway. Every cottage on the rural estate was owned by their employer. Peat for the cottage fires was supplied free of charge, a few shillings weekly were cropped from an already meagre wage, to cover the rental. This deduction left their father very little money to rear twelve children and provide extra nourishment for his ailing wife.

Henry Daniels worked as a shepherd and wore the traditional attire of a hundred years ago, woven smock frock, trousers tied below the knee with binder string, stout clogs and a large wide brimmed straw

Waiting at the Mop Fair to be hired.   *Courtesy: Mair Shepherd*

hat to keep off the sun during Summer or snow in Winter time. His tall crook was made from a two inch thick nut stick with a sheep carved on the handle which he'd fashioned himself. On a bleak Winter night or when a thunder storm threatened to break, the children would hear the rickety stairs creak and the back door bolt being drawn.

'We knew Father was off to the pastures to see if the flock were safe. He was a conscientious man and I often thought he cared more about his sheep than his family', said Stan.

Some land owners allowed shepherds of long standing to run their own sheep with the main flock but Stan couldn't be certain if this happened in his father's case.

As a small boy one of Stan's earliest recollections was of the Mop Fair usually held at Michaelmas, where labourers and craftsmen seeking new masters, lined up in the market square waiting to be hired. Each man wore a symbol indicating his stock-in-trade and the boys played a game of guessing what the symbols stood for. Waggoners tucked a twisted piece of whipcord in their hats, Thatchers displayed strands of woven straw in their lapels, shepherds carried crooks and so on. Land owners liked to hire married men, preferably with sons old enough to help in the fields. Wives could earn 7p or 8p for working a ten hour day in the fields but during harvest time the rate escalated to 2/- daily. Workers were paid 1/9d a day for back breaking chores like lifting potatoes, while the pay for a full day's weeding, carried out by labourer's children was 9d.

On being hired, the oral contract between farm worker and employer was sealed by handing over one shilling followed by a drink at the local public house. This holiday was usually the only day off in the farming year and eagerly looked forward to by the children.

Maids seeking employment lined up in the same way as the men but as each carried a mop, there was no point in proceeding with the guessing game. The array of mops on display accounted for the gathering being called a Mop Fair, a name which has persisted to the present day. A few weeks ago, I spent a wonderful day out attending the annual Mop Fair at Tewkesbury, where stall holders dressed up in Victorian costumes. My delight knew no bounds when I noticed a number of men in traditional garb wearing tokens in their labels exactly as Stan had described.

There were many other side shows to interest young boys at the Mop Fair. The fighting booth for example, where volunteers could spar up against hardy fist-fighters to entertain the people in general. Stalls selling handmade wooden pop guns and birds on sticks were besieged by youngsters with a penny to spend. Girls crowded round stalls displaying ribbons, laces, lavender pouches and butterfly brooches made from gold wire and tiny coloured beads.

Market traders selling pickles, sweetmeats, fruit and vegetables had decorated the grass verge with colourful bunting to attract buyers, but young Stan and his schoolmates were more interested in a stall selling lemonade.

Swing boats were a great favourite with the older children but little ones looked forward to a penny ride on a Dobby Horse. This circle of wooden horses suspended from an overhead rail was operated manually by turning a large handle.

Henry Daniels was a much feared disciplinarian when it came to meting out punishment, so the children had to do exactly as they were told or suffer the consequences. Stan's eldest sister took care of their mother while everyone else had special chores alloted to them daily in and outside the house.

'My job was chopping sticks very early each morning ready for one of my older brothers to light the fire. If by some mishap I was late rising and the sticks were not ready by the grate, father had no qualms about stopping my halfpenny pocket money until I learned my lesson. I played with a spinning top after school but there was always a job to do when I arrived home. As boys we were expected to help father dip and shear the sheep. Many of the sheep suffered from foot rot or worms and we boys would hold them down while father did the necessaries. Whatever went wrong, he would know exactly what to do, in fact, Lord Roundway, was heard to remark, that father was as good, if not better than any vet.

Owing to his vast knowledge of sheep, Henry Daniels wrote a book about the art of shepherding. There was great publicity in Warminster, Devises and Salisbury but the book never got published.

Sometimes newly born lambs were brought home and kept warm in the oven and Stan's sisters would feed them with watered-down milk. When they were strong enough to return to the flock the girls would cry to see their pets being taken away, knowing one day that they'd end up in the local slaughter house.

As he grew older, Stan was trusted to look after their garden which was sizeable in comparison with their cottage. This gave him much pleasure plus a measure of responsibility. First, Stan planted a patch of Sweet William because they gave off a lovely smell, next he filled an ugly bare corner with blackcurrant, redcurrant, and gooseberry bushes. Soon every spare spot was planted with either flowers, vegetable or rhubarb clumps.

Alas the lovely flower beds, the fully established vegetable garden, the mature apple and plum trees, were all left behind when Stan joined the army. In 1920 the Daniel family moved to Merthyr Tydfil, South Wales and the cottage was taken over by new tenants.

Lena Daniels
born 4th April, 1901

Lena was an only child and very reserved in her way. She remembers seeing Stan at their mixed school, but never really conversed with him, not even when his sisters took her to their home after school.

'Probably the five years difference in our ages accounted for Stan not being particularly interested in me. I was just a little girl who played with his sisters and a shy one at that. Of course things changed when Stan began to notice I was not a little girl any longer.'

Being shy, Lena hardly ever went along to barn dances or magic lantern shows held at the village hall. Instead she spent the time doing chores like cleaning and filling the oil lamps at home or finishing off her assignment for the Headmistress of the village school.

Instead of learning her lessons like the rest of the class, Lena spent the whole of her school day knitting stockings and fine cotton collars for Londoners, who were prepared to pay good prices for her excellent work. Over the years, a great deal of money passed hands but the young girl never received a brass farthing for all her hard work.

'Beside the hours I spent knitting, there was also Grandma's home to clean and provisions to collect. That's why I seldom found time for other recreation like dancing or whatever. Owing to mother having to take up full time service I was obliged to move in with Grandma who survived on 2/- a week from the Parish. We ate plain food like cabbage, potatoes and all kinds of vegetables but on Friday I used to order a little meat for Sunday dinner. There wasn't a butcher in the village so the order had to be collected and taken into Warminster ready for the delivery on Saturday when the butcher came in his horse drawn van. I loved my Grandma. She was a gentle, placid person. I don't think she ever got ruffled even during the Spring floods when we were obliged to live upstairs until the yearly Springs were over. Grandma dressed in a long black dress with a tight pleated bodice, over which she wore a snowy white apron, exactly like the little Victorian ladies we see in story books.

I was intrigued to learn more about the yearly Springs. Water rose from the ground at a certain time of year, flooding the village and cottages. The water would appear from no-where and slowly begin to cover the main road. While the water was only a few inches deep, it was just possible for the children, by taking a detour through the fields, to reach the school house at the other end of the village.

'It was great fun avoiding the water until it started to rise more quickly. When that happened it was impossible to go out at all.

Nothing the villagers did could stop the water pouring into the cottages, and there were days of mopping up when the floods receded. I used to wonder why no-one attempted to find other accommodation, knowing full well that the same thing would happen the following Spring. Instead, rather than move away from the danger zone, they were content to carry on mopping up year after year.'

The village children made a point of getting to school early on Shrove Tuesday in order to bar their teacher from entering the building till he promised them the day off.

Whit Monday was the only holiday Lena liked because a Maypole with loads of coloured streamers dangling from the top, was set up on the village green.

Whit. Monday on our village green.

'We each held a streamer and danced in a circle round and round the pole. By weaving in and out, the streamers would criss cross on the pole, covering it with a mass of colour.

One way the boys got the girls to notice them, was by having a go at striking the hammer, but it was impossible for a lad of ten or twelve, to ring the bell. The indicator needed to reach the top mark on the pole before the bell rang and it took a very strong man to win the prize. The prize was usually a kiss from the showman's fat wife.

'But the winner usually had other ideas', said Lena with a smile. 'He'd rather kiss some pretty girl in the crowd, whom he'd chase around the field. The girl would pretend she didn't want to be kissed and we'd run behind goading the fellow on until he finally grabbed and kissed her. But it ended up with the girl's father, landing a real stunner on the cheeky chap's earhole'.

Morris Dancers with bells tied to their legs and wrists came from surrounding towns on these special occasions and were given free beer and bread with cheese for entertaining the crowd.

When the Fair came to Warminster.

From November on, the village choir spent nights rehearsing a special anthem to be sung during the Christmas Eve Candle Procession in which everyone carried a lighted candle. The procession ended at the pub where rum was drunk as long as the candles lasted. When the last candle went out, it was considered time for the unsteady procession to disband.

Cheapjacks displayed their wares on the roadside, used a cloth painted with stars or arctic scenes, as a back drop for displaying crockery, and tinware. Dealers like the oilman visited regularly owing to every home needing parrafin.

'Another familiar sight', said Lena, 'was a big red-bearded man who supplied the cobbler, along with the villagers who tapped their own shoes. The packman also came from time to time with his big brown bag of fancy aprons, scarves, ladies' bloomers and lengths of calico for skirts and dresses'.

Lena remembers the village blacksmith because he told wonderful stories about his experiences as a drummer boy in the Battle of Waterloo and it was at his smithy, that Lord Roundway's horses were shod.

Residents living in very isolated spots were unable to leave their home during bad weather or heavy snow so they relied entirely on the Penny Post to keep them in touch with relatives in distant towns.

Lena left school at 14 to work in Warminster but soon found new employment in a fairly large house in Devon. Her mistress was quite rich and wanted a maid capable of cleaning, cooking, waiting on tables, plus the general household management. The salary offered was £4 monthly, out of which Lena had to buy two uniforms. Duties started at 7am when Lena had to light the stove ready to cook breakfast. After a general tidy up of the kitchen, the main rooms and upstairs had to be cleaned before Mrs. McCreal's daughter and grand daughter arrived for lunch.

'I always changed from my grey morning dress into a blue dress, white apron and cap ready to wait on my Mistress and her family'. There was so much work to do that I plucked up courage to ask for sixpence rise in my pay'.

'Be thankful you are so well off, my girl', was the reply.

Mrs. McCreal entertained lavishly and it was up to Lena to make sure everything was in order before the guests arrived. Some were very famous people who Lena had heard of but hadn't been lucky to see at close range until now.

'Although the majority were gentry and the rest stinking rich, not once did I have to complain of indecent behaviour from flamboyant young rakers or silly old men in their dotage. In fact every one treated me with the utmost respect and though fit to drop I enjoyed every moment'.

One day, Lena discovered to her great joy that an old school friend had been hired to work in a residence quite near. On her next day off she made it her business to contact Mary. From that day forward their time off was spent in each others company either by exploring the Devonshire countryside or making tea alternately in their quarters. By knowing the same people, the girls found a wide variety of topics to talk about but the conservation invariably centred on family left behind in Warminster. A trip home was far too expensive on their small wages. Instead, they'd exchange newsy cards and letters received from village friends telling who was engaged, married or dead since last time of meeting.

'I can't think of anything more to tell you from then on because I got married when I was still working for Mrs. McCreal and it seemed pointless to give up my job when Stan was away in the forces.'

Thanking them both for taking their time I joined the rest of the work group while Stan and Lena prepared for their afternoon nap.

Lena and Stan share a comfortable double room in the Gurnos Residential Home where they are lovingly cared for.

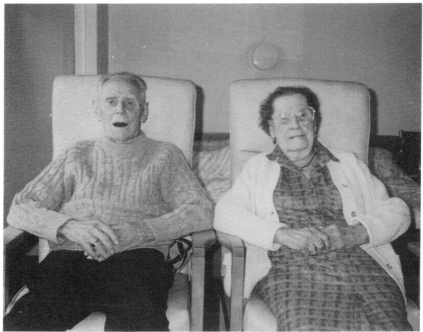

Togetherness at the Gurnos Home. Lena and Stan Daniels

Rebecca Reach
born 25th January, 1903

Rebecca was the oldest of four girls and five boys, living in the Triangle, Pentrebach. With such a large family, their mother found it hard to satisfy the healthy appetites of nine growing children on a colliers wages.

Breakfast was a sparse meal of toast and margarine with the occasional half egg. Nevertheless, their mother made sure the children would have a cooked meal on arriving home from school at 4pm.

'I can't remember ever having meat during weekdays but sometimes on a Sunday there'd be rabbit if one of the boys had been ferreting. Dinners mainly consisted of boiled cabbage because we had a cabbage patch in the back garden. The second vegetable, if there happened to be a second, depended on whatever was cheap and plentiful at that season. We never saw a dish of butter on the table but as we were used to bread spread with margarine, it didn't matter one way or the other. At least Mam saw we had a hot meal daily, which was more than some of our friends had. Any left over bread was made into bread pudding, but that was on very rare occasions, because we usually scoffed the lot with our dinner.'

When I asked Rebecca how much pocket money she received and what she spent it on, she rattled off a long list beginning with NO.

'No pocket money, no chocolate, no pictures, no rides to Merthyr, no trips to seaside, no holidays in short No to any or everything that cost money. There was the odd occasion, when Mam bought a bag of mixed sweets on tick, from the corner shop, and gave us one each to go to school'.

'What did you do in your spare time?', I inquired.

'Scrubbed and sanded our flagstone floor, cleaned the windows, dusted the crockery on the dresser, helped Fanny with the cleaning, fed, washed and dressed my younger sisters and if there was time left before going to bed, played ball in Long Row. Some mornings before school started, I helped other children to clean Pentrebach School or carry coal in ready for teacher to light the stove. During weekends and school holidays we all played by the brook, nicknamed the Feeder. Our parents were very strict about playing with the boys, we were continuously warned of playing Hanky Panky and I had many a hiding through no fault of my own. Not one of us dared answer our parents back or we'd have a clip around the ear'.

There was a low bridge over the feeder and a favourite game with

The famous Triangle, Pentrebach, Merthyr, where Rebecca Reach was born and bred.

the children was hanging as far over as safety would allow, but the boys not content to watch from the bank, used to run across and push the girls into the brook. There were the occasions when Rebecca went home soaking wet and received a good hiding through no fault of her own, beside which she was sent to bed without a drink or anything to eat. Another game was throwing an orange rope over the arm of a lamp post and swinging round until the rope worked its way off the arm. This was a dangerous game as the unfortunate victim ended up on the ground with a nasty bump or something more serious like a broken arm or leg.

'Mind you', laughed Rebecca 'I was as rough and ready as the next and up to all kind of devilment. I loved playing football which certainly isn't very ladylike and could fight as well as any boy. I can remember swinging from a lamp post outside the corner sweet shop late one evening when the children began shouting';

'Jump off Becky, run like hell, Old Bengy's coming down Long Street waving his stick like mad'.

Fortunately Rebecca could outrun the local bobby, but when things went the other way, the bobby wasn't slow in administering punishment on the spot. It was no use running crying to their parents or expecting words of sympathy.

'Serves you right, you must have asked for it', was the usual response.

Hoop-and-stick.

Hoop-and-stick was another popular game but Rebecca had no money to buy one. The publican of the local Inn piled the empty beer barrels every morning in front of the Pub ready for the dray man to collect them. Around the middle of the barrel was a thick metal band and when no-one was looking, the bigger boys would try to force it off. One morning they managed to get the band off one of the barrels before Old Bengy spotted them and gave it to Rebecca.

'The band was never any good as a hoop, because it was shaped to fit the barrel and kept going sideways'.

There was always a lot of gossip going on in the corner shop concerning certain individuals who got themselves into trouble, so bringing shame on their respectable families. Teenagers, overhearing this malicious gossip used to run after the pregnant girl, shouting loudly, -

'Shame on you. Shame on you, you're going to have a baby, you're going to have a baby'.

The wife of the local costerer was a constant topic for discussion with customers at the corner shop. She was a tough character with a number of children. Each time she gave birth, instead of resting up the following day, she'd be back on the coster cart weighing potatoes, as if nothing had happened.

The Triangle was a close knit community with many related families who spoke Welsh and didn't take kindly to strangers. Contrary to their usual treatment of so called 'foreigners', Rebecca's mother who was English, was accepted without question.

'Every night when my father came home from the pit', said Rebecca, 'my brother would carry the tin bath from the sculery, and place it in front of the fire. Mam filled the bath from the iron boiler warming on a roaring fire, so Dad could wash the coal dust off his body before going to bed.'

Each Saturday, it fell to Rebecca to get the thick caked mud off her father's working boots before rubbing them over with oil to keep the leather supple.

'Dad went from bed to work. I don't remember seeing him in any other but his working clothes, except on one sad occasion. It was the funeral of my brother Tom, who was killed in Plymouth colliery a fortnight after starting work underground. Beside being handsome and well built, our Tom was a lovely thoughful boy and Mam idolised every inch of her 6 ft 5 inch giant. I can tell you this for certain, it all but broke our Mam's heart when my brother died so young'.

Another sad occasion Rebecca recalls, concerned a young lad living near them in the Triangle. After buying a motor bike, he decided it was safer to keep it indoors in case someone seeing it propped against the wall, would be tempted to take it for a spin.

'Goodness only knows what happened, but somehow the bike caught fire and all the family burned to death. The villagers were sick with shock to learn what had taken place in the early hours of the

When a whole village respected the dead. Family walked before the coffin - friends and neighbours behind. Courtesy: Bill Jones. Welsh Industrial & Maritime Museum Cardiff.

morning while they were fast asleep. We all walked behind the coffins. There wasn't a dry eye in the whole of Pentrebach that day.'

'We never had much in the way of material goods, you could say we had the bare essentials, a tin bath and a paraffin lamp that was about all. As children we slept in one room with our beds pushed together against the wall in case we fell out but it didn't make us better or worse than the next person. Ours was a home full of love, laughter and companionship, things that are sadly lacking in the world at present. Where we had nothing and were happy, the children today seem to have everything they ask for and are still discontented'.

As for 90 year old Rebecca, she counts her blessings for two reasons. Not only is she fortunate in having regular visits from her family but is also surrounded by the friends she's made at her new home.

Rebecca Reach

George Hanney
born 6th August, 1908

George, was the eldest of five children born to Jonathan Hanney a stone mason living at Ernest Street, Merthyr. I was interested to learn that the first house built in Milbourne Terrace, Merthyr, was for the Hanney family. Even more interesting is the fact that the building from the day it was first occupied over a hundred years ago has remained a Hanney possession. When other houses were built either side of the once solitary dwelling, it became number 4 Milbourne Terrace. At the time of writing, Mr. Ken Hanney, youngest of the four brothers resides there with his wife Dorothy.

From the time he was old enough to hold a pencil, infant George was forever scribbling things on his little slate with coloured chalks. By the age of five, he was able to capture the likeness of objects, flowers and toys. Every room in their house had a drawing or two pinned on the wall and shortly after the little boy started school, the classroom walls were quickly covered with drawings by this gifted lad. Later, when given his first box of paints and a paint brush, there was no holding him back.

'There were paintings everywhere you looked, my mother was so proud of my winning prizes and she made sure every award was given a place of honour in our parlour'.

Things were tough for the family when Jonathan Hanney, still in his prime, died, leaving four sons and a daughter to be reared on a widow's pension which was barely enough to feed let alone clothe the children.

Cyril and Vivian, twin sons, went off to Canada on a farming community scheme. When War broke out, Cyril joined the Canadian Church Army, and after the war ended, he continued in the service of the Lord, reaching the esteemed position of Canon. He was also a zealous supporter of any campaign aimed to counteract drug addiction. Cyril's undeterred drive plus heartfelt compassion for the drug addicted and people without hope, forced him to travel as far afield as Mexico. In 1942, Canon Cyril Hanney, returned to Merthyr for the first time after sixteen long years away from home and family.

During the visit, he was invited to take the Sunday Service at the Church of St. David, High Street, Merthyr.

Vivian, his twin brother, joined the Canadian Army and was killed the day before the Armistice was signed. He was buried with full military honours in the country he'd chosen to be his home.

From 1947 onwards, after the war years, George became a well known figure in art circles. His brilliant illustrations, cartoons, water colour landscapes and portraits in oil were exhibited in galleries etc. Drawings depicting 'The Crouched Trek to the Coal Face', 'The Cwbs', 'The Old Iron Bridge', 'Merthyr Market', 'Harry the Black', 'John Morgan's Bun Fight', are but a small example of George Hanney's outstanding talent.

Art classes conducted by George, were held at Queen's Road School for youths interested in painting. His secular employment was designing toys at the Triang Factory on the old Cyfarthfa Works site and it was there, George designed a special perambulator for Hazel, his daughter-in-law, who was expecting triplets.

He also taught art for many years at both Brecon and Merthyr College's of Further Education and was appointed Chairman of the local Art Society as well as becoming Chairman of the Music Society. Being so much in demand, George, opened a studio above Burton the Tailor, and owing to its great success, he moved his studio to larger premises on top of the Provincial Bank.

One day he was commissioned by the proprietor of the Manchester House to paint a large mural on the upstair wall of the children's department. Christmas was getting near and one end of the department was going to be converted into a grotto for Santa Claus.

George painted a spectacular Christmas scene in which Santa Claus was surrounded by a crowd of little children telling him what presents they wanted him to drop down their chimney on Christmas morning.

The Manchester House as such is no longer trading and like most old establishments has seen many changes take place under various types of management. At present a Furniture Company occupies the premises but not to be outdone, I made it my business to inquire if the mural was still visible on the upper stair wall.

It appeared that the mural was still in excellent condition when the management prior to the present furnishing company, took possession of the premises. Like most old buildings, it was badly in need of repair. Orders to go ahead with a complete new face lift, were sent from head office and quickly executed. In the process, George's wonderful mural was painted over to fit in with the rest of the smart decor.

Words are inadequate to describe my disappointment as I walked from the furniture store. Nevertheless, I have ben privileged to have one of George's well known drawings entitled, 'John Morgan's Bunn Fight', for the cover of this book. Also a number of his interesting drawings can be seen on the pages following.

My grateful thanks go to Mr. Geoffrey Hanney and his wife Hazel, for giving me permission to have several copies made of the artist's most treasured and valuable collection.

Recently, owing to failing health, George joined the Gurnos Home Family.

Mrs. Margo Pugh, Officer in Charge, aided by her staff, have hung the drawings and cartoons, on the corridor walls outside George's bedroom. He now has his own Gallery to peruse each day. And if that isn't the kindest way of showing empathy for residents in their care, then I'd like to know what is !!

Disaster at the Pit.

Courtesy: George Hanney

Dr. Ernie Ward and his 'Yellow Peril' Sunbeam car.

Courtesy: George Hanney

Miners coming from the 'Cwbs'.

The crouched trek to the coalface.

Merthyr Market before demolition. *Courtesy: George Hanney*

Harry the Black *Courtesy: George Hanney*

Workshop group at Gurnos Home.

Workshop at Gurnos with Officer Margo Pugh standing.

Staff and group at Gurnos.

Relaxing between a work session.

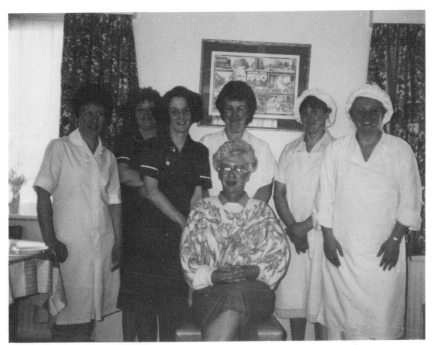

Officer Margo Pugh with her staff.

Sandbrook House, Merthyr Tydfil

The Day Centre at the rear of Sandbrook House.

Courtesy: Meirion Davies

Sandbrook House

Sandbrook is a spacious Residential Home overlooking Merthyr town. It stands in three acres of ground, its gardens aglow with colour throughout the seasons, while high walls and impressive iron gates give additional prestige to the stately residence.

I was quite interested to learn that Sandbrook House was previously known by a different name, so out of curiosity I began to piece together a brief history of Brynteg House as it was then called.

It was to this lovely house that Griffith Llewellyn brought his young bride Miss Lilian Sandbrook the daughter of Mr. Simon Sandbrook a well known and much respected Ironmonger. Not only was Simon Sandbrook recognised for his keen business sense but also for the distinguished part played throughout the years in public life and affairs of Merthyr. His well stocked store occupied the site in Glebelands Street where Threshers Wine Shop now stands just a few doors from the Belle View Hotel which fortunately has survived the years of change and unforeseen circumstances.

While chatting with Mrs. Eirwen McDonald of Tudor Street, Merthyr, I found she left Heolgerrig School at fifteen and went to work as a kitchen maid in Brynteg House.

'I was thrilled on seeing Brynteg for the first time. It seemed massive compared to ordinary street dwellings and as it was Summertime the gardens were a mass of bright colour. In addition to magnificent lawns, there were fruit trees and kitchen gardens. On entering the house, wasn't I glad that Mrs. Llewellyn had engaged me!!'

Every room was tastefully furnished but the room that most impressed young Eirwen was the wonderful oak panelled library with its row upon row of expensive leather bound volumes and unique parquet floor. The dining room was also very elegant but oddly enough with the exception of two items the silver was kept hidden away in the cupboard of the large oak sideboard.

'Most people would flaunt it but they weren't the sort to show off', remarked Eirwen.

The upstairs bathroom had one of those lovely big baths you could stretch out in, there was also a toilet and hand basin in the downstair cloakroom plus an outdoor lavatory for the servants. Cooking was done on the kitchen range but in case of emergency, a gas cooker was installed in the scullery.

Eirwen, a chubby girl with short straight hair thought she was the cat's whiskers, in her red and white striped dress, plain white apron and cap minus frills. The position included board and lodge, a free

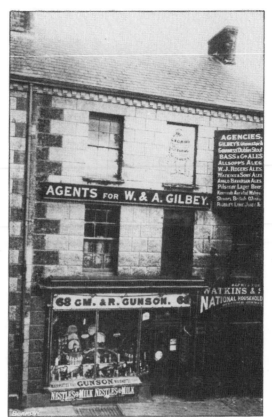

G. M. & R. GUNSON,

FAMILY GROCERS,

Tea, Coffee and Italian Warehousemen,

WINE AND SPIRIT MERCHANTS,

67 and 68, High Street, Merthyr Tydfil.
(Opposite Post Office)

uniform, plus a weekly salary of five shillings which increased with length of service. She shared a room with the 'between maid', but when the Llewellyns moved away to Cardiff, Eirwen went with them and was allocated a room for herself. Duties at Brynteg House commenced at 7.30 sharp, and Eirwen was up early lighting the kitchen range and preparing things ready to cook. Her next chore was cleaning, laying and lighting both sitting and dining room fires after which the 'between maid' helped in dusting the downstairs rooms. Everything that needed doing that day had to be finished by lunch time. The servants had their meals at a different time from the family and each afternoon, both parlour and between maids changed into brown dresses with fancy aprons and matching caps. As Eirwen helped cook in the afternoons, just the one uniform was sufficient but later on when graduating to between maid, a second uniform was given her. Eirwen was given two half days weekly, either Wednesday and Saturday or Thursday and Sunday with a verbal warning to be back indoors by ten o'clock sharp.

The Family Butcher.   *Courtesy: Merthyr Public Libraries*

'General provisions were ordered from Gunson the high class grocer of the day and as there were no fridges the meat was delivered fresh each day from Williams the High Street butcher. The delivery boy beside being about my own age, was very good looking and popular with the kitchen staff. Cook said he deserved a cup of cocoa and a bite to eat for dragging his bike all the way up the steep hill.'

I found out to my surprise, that the young good looking butcher's boy, who delivered fresh meat to Brynteg House, was no other than Reg Clayton, my husband's uncle. He's over eighty now and still going strong, probably due to Eirwen's cups of cocoa. I asked whether he remembered what price the Llewellyns paid for meat.

'Of course I remember', said Uncle Reg, 'best sausages were ten pennies a pound, lamb fry one shilling, a cow's heart sixpence and half a crown would buy a whole sirloin of beef but I don't think we'll ever see those prices again, they're gone for good.'

Assuming that Mrs. Lilian Llewellyn would buy her clothes from B. Harris Jones or one of the other excellent ladies outfitters in Merthyr, I was interested to learn, that her personal wardrobe was ordered from a select store in Queen Street, Cardiff.

Mrs. Llewellyn's satin garments and delicate underwear, were hand washed daily by the parlour maid, but uniforms, bed linen and general washing was sent to the laundry to be washed, dried and ironed.

Griffith and Lilian Llewellyn spent a fortnight each year in the country during which time the house was locked up and the staff sent home. The head gardener lived on the premises so there was no fear of someone breaking in while the owners were on vacation. This also meant that lawns, flower beds, fruit trees and kitchen gardens were properly maintained while the owners were away.

'Except for their golf and occasional entertaining, the Llewellyns were more or less home birds and very good employers. Mrs. Llewellyn was very kind to the staff and at Christmastime gave each one of us a nice present and extra wages.'

At that time Merthyr badly needed a hospital school where the growing number of rheumatic children would not only receive treatment as residents but be able to keep up their studies.

Griffith Llewellyn's offices were situated in Victoria Street which was conveniently close to Brynteg House but later when a partnership was formed with Mr. Hann a fellow solicitor, it was more convenient because of the nature of the business, to operate from Cardiff instead of Merthyr. Eirwen well remembers her employer's words on deciding to leave the home he loved.

'If Brynteg had wheels it would be in Cardiff'

Knowing full well how desperately the borough needed a Hospital School for children suffering from rheumatic fever, Griffith Llewellyn presented Brynteg House as a gift to Merthyr Education Committee.

The Hospital School was formally opened on September 16th, 1937 by Mrs. Llewellyn and on her husband's wish their former residence was renamed 'Sandbrook House'. Lilian Llewellyn was said to be deeply moved by the kind thoughtful gesture of her husband in suggesting the new hospital school should be named in memory of Simon Sandbrook. I quote her final words when performing the opening ceremony.

'I cannot help feeling how proud my father would have been had he known that this hospital school would have borne his name'.

In 1974 Sandbrook House became a Residential Home for the Elderly.

Brynteg House - when it became Sandbrook Rheumatic Hospital.

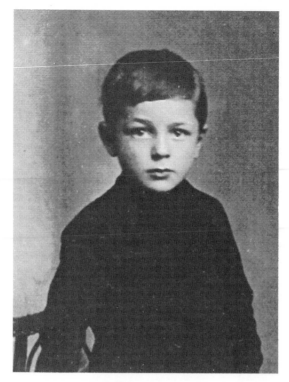

Ossie Jones
born 17th May, 1913

Ossie was the smallest of eight or maybe ten children born to Belinda and Evan Jones, High Street, Penydarren. Ossie has a faint recollection of two children being buried when he was about three or four years old, otherwise his memory is clear regarding the eight surviving members of the large family.

At the tender age of six, Ossie was out of bed by five thirty and while it was still dark, he'd be pacing the street with a bundle of newspapers to catch early shift steel workers on their way to Dowlais Works.

'Penny penny, get your penny paper', was his spiel.

Old Mr. Tanner gave him three halfpennies for every dozen papers sold but Ossie made sure the papers handed to him included the Merthyr Express it being the most popular and quickest to sell. Once school was over, after a quick bite to eat, he'd be down the road like a long dog, to collect a stack of Echos from Polly the Post. This time instead of being alone Ossie joined up with Polly's two daughters, Eira and Muriel for the evening distribution.

'Everyone wanted the Echo those days, the demand was too much for one paper boy to contend with', said Ossie. 'I also remember running uphill all the way from Penydarren to the Antelope Station Dowlais Top with three or four brown paper parcels tied with string and sealed with red wax. I'd get there just as the Abergavenny train was about to leave, my breath would be in my fist and my boot studs sparking as I raced along the platform'.

There was no stopping Ossie at this point of our discussion, so I sat back and listened with amusement as he continued.

'My sister Phyllis who was only fifteen at the time, went into service with Lord and Lady Hill. Their mansion happened to be in Abergavenny so it was easy for me to call at the big house whenever Polly the Post sent me to deliver parcels. Everybody living in that area was posh even the servants, and I was told to use the back entrance whenever I wanted to see Phyllis. The cook was very stiff and starchy but she never let me leave Lord Hill's without a small food parcel for our Mam and a chunk of bread pudding to eat on the train'.

A dozen or more houses at the bottom of Penydarren High Street were very small. After opening the low front door which was on street level, there were two or three indoor steps leading down to an underground living room. A tiny back window looking towards Penyard gave a little light but in order to see clearly an oil lamp was kept burning most of the day and well into the small hours of the morning. Probably many of the chronic chest cases in those days were due to unhealthy oil fumes in those airless hovels.

The reason Ossie remembered the small houses was because of a character called Gwen Rowlands whose left leg was six inches shorter than the right one. Gwen wore a special thick wedged lace up shoe with an unsightly heel. Lots of people who were lame from birth or disabled by accident instead of having surgery to put things right, wore a special built up shoe similar to hers.

'But Gwen was different from the others, except for the big shoe, she was dainty, pretty and very kind to me', said Ossie. 'I suffered untold agonies when my schoolmates shouted 'One down and carry one', or 'Hop a long Gwenny', and mimicked the way she walked.'

An old friend of Ossie's father, was involved in a serious accident underground and reported to be buried alive in a section cut off by the fall. Three days later the rescue team succeeded in cutting through and to their amazement found the miner alive and no worse from his ordeal. In keeping with the Welsh tradition, he was known from that day onward as Dai Dead.

The Jones family attended the Radcliff Hall on Sundays it then being

A common sight during the depression. Picking coal from amongst the colliery waste.

Courtesy: Bill Jones. Welsh Industrial & Maritime Museum Cardiff.

the main place of worship and as a reward for regular attendance, the children went each year on the annual Sunday school trip to Pontsarn.

'We always had food in the Pontsarn Pavilion. After we finished lunch, there were competitive events in the field behind the pavilion and packets of boiled sweets for the winners. Sack and three legged races were popular with boys and girls but I preferred the egg and spoon race because I always won. When the games were over we'd sit beneath the Viaduct and share the boiled sweets or maybe dam a shallow part of the river where we could swim in our pants. If there were no girls about we'd jump in naked praying our Sunday School Superintendant didn't catch us. When the weather was chilly, we'd wander down to the Blue Pool hoping someone was about to commit suicide. Dozens of people ended their lives by jumping off the narrow stone bridge high above the deep black water of the Blue Pool. It was very frightening but I always went along with the boys or they'd call me a Cowardly Custard.'

Another Summer Outing was a ride by tramcar to Cyfarthfa Park, paid and organised by John Morgan founder of the Ragged Sunday School. That was a day of days because all amusements within the park like swing boats, or pony and donkey rides were absolutely free. Each child received a lunch pack, an apple, a packet of sweets, a cornet from Sidoli's cart and a whole shilling to spend.

When John Morgan became ill, there was a continuous stream of children in Church Street, Merthyr waiting their turn to visit him. A few children at a time, were allowed into the bedroom where John Morgan lay in a big four poster bed. This probably accounted for the number of well wishers.

Large families were resigned to live in small houses with two or in many instances, only one bedroom. This resulted in three, four or maybe more children sharing beds. If it happened that a father and his sons worked different shifts in the pit or steel works, as one would be leaving home another would be coming from work. The old saying that beds in such a home never had time to get cold, proved in this case to be true. Considering the cramped conditions in many homes those days, it's not surprising that a grand four poster bed with just one occupant was a rare sight indeed to the children.

'Sometimes money was so tight that Dad's friends had to go to Dewi Sant or Dick Jones Garden City, to ask for help off the Parish, but it was easier to get blood from a stone. To keep warm in Winter, gangs of men would go up the patches searching for small coal and when the sacks were full, wheel it all the way down hill to Penydarren in a barrow without brakes. Things were not easy by a long chalk but we

Picking coal from The Patches.   Courtesy: Bill Jones. Welsh Industrial & Maritime Museum Cardiff.

Courtesy: Bill Jones. Welsh Industrial & Maritime Museum Cardiff.

Digging among the snow. But it was worthwhile for a bag of coal to keep the home fires burning.

had to be content with our lot and I for one wouldn't mind being back there again'.

Like most boys, Ossie was wicked and one of his favourite tricks was to bore a hole in a shilling just big enough to thread some cotton through. If someone was walking down the pavement, the shilling was put in a prominent spot where it was sure to be seen and Ossie would hide in a doorway. Making sure no-one was watching, the person would bend quickly to pocket the coin, at that exact moment Ossie would pull the thread making the coin disappear.

Strong horses and weak donkeys.

Courtesy: George Hanney

Popular games like marbles, pitch and toss, strong horses and weak donkeys or catty dog, were played in all school yards but Ossie was told by his Dad that pitch and toss was really gambling and if the police caught small boys playing for money they would be put in jail.

'I hated the thought of going to the dentist because my friend Eddie Milktins told me what happened when the dentist had you helpless in his chair. Eddie had a halfpenny for beating a number of empty condensed milk tins tied together with cord. During an extraction, at the given signal, Eddie would bang the tins loudly so patients waiting their turn couldn't hear the screams coming from the surgery.'

Election times was very exciting. The Jones family were staunch labour and voted for Wallhead whose face was plastered in every window for days before the election. There was always someone in opposition though it didn't mean they were of a different party.

Ossie broke into a little ditty he sang at election time.

Wallhead is a gentleman
Fox Davies is a fool
Instead of going to Parliament
He ought to go to school

He also remembers another candidate for Parliament opposing Wallhead and buying votes by giving away food parcels. Election results took a long time to reach the public and sometimes the crowd would wait until 2 or 3am of a morning outside the Town Hall to hear whether their favourite had 'Got In'.

'Bradley Birt's parcels didn't do him much good', chuckled Ossie, 'because good old Wallhead walked it with a big majority'.

Then came a second ditty.

Vote, vote, vote for Mr. Wallhead
You won't find a better man
We'll all vote for him
then we'll try to get him in
And put old Bradley Birt upon the floor

When Merthyr Iron Works were in full production the population was 89,000 and Wallhead had a 33,000 majority gain over all parties. Mr. S.O. Davies the Miners Agent stood for Parliament when Wallhead died and got in without any problem.

Ossie sang the ditty once more, this time, with a slight variation for Mr. S.O. Davies the new candidate.

Vote, vote, vote for S.O. Davies
You won't find a better man
We'll all vote for him
to try to get him in
and we'll hang his opposers
On the pole

Elections were fun on the whole but there were bound to be the odd fight among the more fiery headed. A circle would be formed leaving plenty of space for the two opponents and bets quickly placed on the likely winner. They were always man to man, fist to fist, and shake hands at the finish fights, not like today when men use their boots and flick knives. Then there'd be a free for all, which would end with everyone making for the pub and the fighters arming each other like long lost brothers.

'We mixed well with the Spaniards', said Ossie, 'you'd never find one of them suffering from T.B. which was a killer when I was growing up. When I asked a Spanish boy the reason he told me his mother used to go looking for a certain kind of snail which she left overnight in a basin of water. In the morning the family would drink the slimy liquid which protected them against the dreadful disease.'

People in Penydarren used to say that Jews were mean and money grabbing but Ossie proved that was not true in the case of old Mr. Giddlestone from Garden City. When Ossie's sister Blodwen was very ill, the old man used to send six eggs and a few shillings to his mother each week to buy nourishing food for the sick girl.

On Christmas Lord Buckland used to donate ten shillings to the old people and Ossie remembers queuing outside old Elim Chapel at the bottom of North Street, Penydarren to collect the money for his parents.

Ossie was admitted to Sandbrook House in 1984 because his sister being blind was unable to care for him any longer and is very happy among people he's come to call his new family.

Ossie Jones

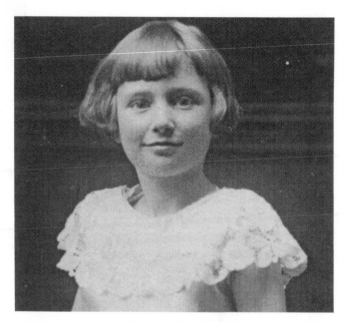

Lucy Smith
born 27th November, 1903

Lucy was one of nine children, eight sisters and one brother. Their Dad was a Road Man underground and later found a job for his son in the same pit with dire consequences. Shortly after his eighteenth birthday, the boy broke his back when the pit props collapsed and he died along with many of his workmates.

One of Lucy's first recollections are of a childrens ward in the Mardy Isolation Hospital Merthyr where she spent many unhappy weeks. Scarlet fever was rampant in the valleys at that time and as antibiotics and other miracle drugs were unheard of, scores of young lives were lost. All wards were crammed to capacity owing to the epidemic, as a result the nurses were rushed off their feet. Fortunately for Lucy, one of her older sisters was employed as a ward cleaner and with the situation being so bad, was allowed to nurse and look after Lucy personally.

To prevent spreading the infection to others, all visitors had to stay outside in the hospital grounds and comfort their children through closed windows of the ward. As you can well imagine each visit caused chaos and misery for parents and patients alike. Neither were visitors able to visit daily but only at stipulated times.

Inside a ward at The Mardy Isolation Hospital.

'Mammy and my sisters used to cry when the bell rang to show it was time to leave, and like all the other children in the ward, I used to scream my head off for hours after they'd left. When we'd begin to settle down a bit it was time again for visiting and our screams could be heard in the houses outside the gates. As I began to get better I'd wait at the window behind my bed to see what Mammy had brought me. Once I had a licorice basket and another time, a sweet sugar pig. Daddy used to be very upset if I cried and I remember him saying;

'If you are a good girl and don't cry, I'll buy you a doll when you come home'.

'Can't you bring it here for me to play with Daddy?', I asked him.

'No lovely, because you'd have to leave it behind and a doll costs a lot of hard earned money'.

'Of course', said Lucy, 'I had to cry a bit in case Mammy thought I didn't love her anymore but Daddy kept his promise and there was a china doll on my bed when I arrived home'.

'My family lived in a three bedroomed house in Bryn Street, Twynyrodyn which meant four of us girls shared two beds in one bedroom, and the others had my brother in with them', Lucy said. 'The rooms were stark and cold specially when the snow came, but we had stone bottles filled with boiling water to warm the beds until we got off to sleep'.

Lucy talked about a typical day when she was seven or eight. The children got up no later than seven thirty a.m. and took it in turn to wash under the cold water tap in the back kitchen. Beneath the tap was a bucket to catch the water. Breakfast consisted of thick slices of bread toasted on a fork in front of the open fire. But in Winter they received a basin of thick lumpy porridge sweetened with honey.

They didn't have far to go to Twynyrodyn School as it was at the top of their street. Even so, Lucy and one of her sisters was always there by eight thirty. Believe it or not but the children went early in order to help the cleaners carry heavy buckets of coal ready to light the classroom stove.

'It took two of us ages to carry the buckets from the coal house', said Lucy, 'most times the bell would be ringing for class before we finished'. That wasn't the end of their chores by a long way, as Lucy went on to explain.

'Our back kitchen was flag stoned and when we came home from school dinner time, Mammy would have removed the rag mats and our job was to scrub the floor with a block of hard soap then sprinkle it with sand. The rag mats were made from left over pieces of material or strips of old clothing woven into a sugar or flour sack. All the family spent hours every evening making rag mats, it was our entertainment.'

Punishing was more frequently applied those days although in most cases the offence was trivial. For a reason she couldn't recall, Lucy was told to go to the headmistress' room. Miss Davies had her office at the front of the school so no-one knew whether the pupils turned up or not. Lucy decided to hide in the toilet long enough to fool her teacher then went back crying to her classroom. Imagine her horror to see Miss Davies talking to Mrs. Rees. After a bit of quick thinking, the little girl pretended to have fallen in the yard and hurt herself. But Miss Davies wasn't that stupid and demanded to see the injured leg. Of course there wasn't a scratch to be seen on the child's body, so she was marched back to the office and punished for lying.

Lucy like most girls in her class, wore a pinafore with sleeves over her school dress, and black boots which her father tapped himself. She had long fair hair past her shoulders which was usually plaited during school hours to prevent her picking up head lice.

'The girl sitting in front of me was swarming with chickens (head lice), and I could see them running through her hair when she bent down. The cure was to wash the hair in disinfectant, clean the nits off with a steel tooth comb then rub Harrisons Pomade over the scalp.'

Food was home cooked and twice a week Lucy and her sisters carried large tins of bread to the bakehouse opposite the school. Broth seemed to be the staple meal of the day, sometimes made from split peas, lentils or potatoes but to find a piece of meat was a rare treat. Clothes for the children were cut from old coats or other garments and handed down from the oldest to the youngest until they wore out.

After school the children would play in the field where Taff Glen View now stands or play 'Kick the Tin, Skinny Lighto or The Big Ship Sails on the Ally Ally O'. Their father was a nasty man and prone to hitting them hard if they weren't home by eight. He was also an ardent music lover and bought himself a gramophone.

If we made a sound or even whispered when Dad was listening to a record, the one sitting nearest him would receive a whack wherever his hand chanced to fall. If we were very naughty he would make us scrub the kitchen table to save using a table cloth, but if we upset Mammy she'd threaten us with a stick called the Ginney which was guaranteed to raise blisters on our bums.'

Being so many, the children were bathed on different nights. Usually the two youngest went into the tub after each other. A huge iron boiler was filled with cold water which took ages to heat then poured into the tub Dad had placed in front of the fire. More water was boiled ready for the second one, which meant the water would be almost up to the handles of the tub. Lucy bathed after her sister each Friday night, but first their mother went through their heads with a derbac toothcomb to make sure there were no nits. This was a painful experience as the steel comb pulled out bunches of hair. Pity help anyone with curls - it was worse than Chinese torture!!

Even worse, was sitting on the stairs each Saturday morning, waiting for Mam to drain the senna pods out of the saucepan. A cup of lukewarm senna tea was handed to each child, after which, their mother checked the cups.

'It was putrid stuff', said Lucy, 'and I vowed there and then never to give senna tea to my children if I ever had any'.

At the bottom of the street was a house with a shop attached. The owner turned the shop into a chapel where the children could go on Sunday to hear Bible stories. There was no particular denomination or real minister so the adults took turns at reading the scriptures. A couple of hymns were sung and a short prayer given at the end of the meeting. Sometimes there'd be a magic lantern showing baby Moses in the bullrushes or Noah building the ark but the slides were indistinct and the machine kept breaking down.

'If I'd been very good, Mammy would give me a penny to go to the Electric Cinema. The silent black and white pictures were mostly about Cowboys and Indians, with a short serial to be continued the following week. To buck it up a bit, a lady played the piano during fights with the Indians or if the hero was in danger. There were no refreshments sold in the Electric, but as we were skint, it didn't really matter', said Lucy.

When Lucy was twelve years old she earned half a crown weekly for taking customers orders to a grocery store in Twyn and when she left school at fourteen a teacher living in Dyke Street offered to pay her five shillings a week for cleaning his house.

'Girls had little choice other than to go into service for paltry wages or stand behind a counter for ten hours until they found someone to settle down with for life.'

'Divorce was an ugly word, and because everyone went either to church or chapel, they were taught to respect the sanctity of marriage. It was therefore very much a case of, Once Married, Always Married, whatever the situation happened to be. It's so different these days, when you can get a divorce for trivial things like not wanting to watch the same televison programme as your partner or some other stupid reason. On the subject of marriage, I remember how different weddings were back then. Most brides wore a navy, brown or grey suit with a nice silk blouse and a wide brimmed hat. Oftentimes, it was difficult to make out which one was the bride, unless she carried a bouquet, as all the ladies wore suits and a rose or carnation pinned to their collars.'

Courtesy: Glyn Jones

The photograph shown above of a typical wedding group, lends credence to Lucy's accurate recollections of the past era.

Lucy was admitted to Sandbrook House in 1991 where she finds herself surrounded by loving friends who are also grateful for the happy ambience of their pleasant new Home.

Lucy Smith

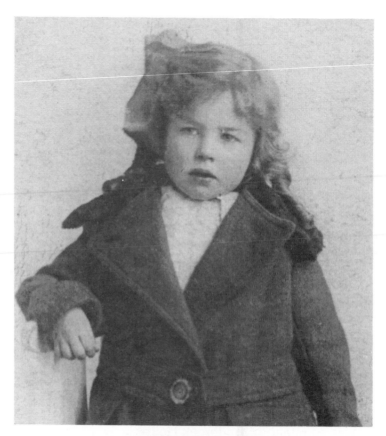

Nell Roberson
born 16th July, 1903

Nell was just a baby when her mother died, leaving her husband Tom and twelve year old Ria, to care for the four children. Their father worked at Ynysfach Steel Works for long hours on end, leaving little leisure time to spend with the children. It fell to young Ria to look after baby Nell, make food for the others and sort out the household chores. Nell remembers back to the day her elder sister got her ready one morning to go to the Infant School.

'Ria washed me under the cold water tap in the pantry, dressed me in my best dress, tied my curls back with ribbons and made sure my shoes were clean. We lived in Williams Town and the Catholic school was at the bottom end of Merthyr. My older brother was fifteen at the time and very strong. Each morning he'd carry me down the British Tip through Merthyr High Street and all the way to school on his back. When school was over I had to wait outside the gate till he came to

The Canal Walk, Merthyr Tydfil

carry me all the way back home.'

Being very small, Nell was a sitting target for school bullies though she was quick to admit that many of the hidings were her own fault.

'I was a very naughty little girl, my seat was behind two classmates with long ringlets. I used to tie the ringlets together and ask teacher to be excused. I'd hide in the Lav and listen to them crying as Miss Jones tried to separate the tangles. Another favourite pastime was knocking doors and running away but one day Auntie Maggie who I really hated, went round the back and saw me kicking her gate with my new boots. First she thumped me then grabbing me by the scruff dragged me screaming blue murder down to the Catholic Church on Brecon Road. I remember there were two Fathers in the church, one was nice and the other nasty, they happened to be brothers so were both called Father Heinze. Auntie Maggie reported me to the nasty one and I was obliged to sit in the confession box and tell him all the naughty things I'd done that week'.

'Repeat five Hail Mary's and don't kick your aunt's door again', was his advice.

By the time Nell arrived home, there wasn't a person in Williams Town who hadn't heard of her misconduct. Worse still, Auntie Maggie went to meet her brother in law on his way from work to tell him what Nell had done.

'He gave me such a wallop, I expected my head to drop off, but I never went near her gate from that day on'.

The sisters shared in doing the housework but when Nell was fed up she'd do a disappearing act.

'You'll find her in the bedroom nursing that stupid cat', Maria would say angrily, and sure enough they'd find Nell nursing the cat in the doll's shawl.

Maria was the delicate one of the family and much of their father's small income was spent on medicines to help cure her ailments but in spite of always being under the weather and lovingly referred to as the 'Creaking Door', Maria survived until she was sixty five year old.

Sometimes during school holidays, the children would have a picnic on the canal bank consisting of pop made from lemon sherbert and whatever was left over in the pantry. During hot weather, the children were tempted to dip their feet in the cool canal water, but were afraid to chance it because of the blood curdling stories passed on by grown ups. The canal was home to a family of 'Water Dogs', who were reported to have bitten off arms, fingers, legs and toes of the more venturesome. It wasn't customary to see the water dogs that early in the day but nevertheless, it was safer to be cautious than go

Horse drawing barge along the tow path on the Merthyr-Cardiff Canal.

home minus a limb. Often times when it was growing dusk, as the children were leaving to go home, they'd hear the odd whistling made by the water dogs underneath the water.

Nell referred on numerous occasions to these vicious animals which were quite unknown to myself, so I decided to spend a day talking to residents living near the canal bank who were likely to remember the water dogs. Imagine my surprise to discover they were simply a family of otters living in the Rhydcar section of the old canal.

'You should have asked me', said my husband, 'I knew all about the water dogs as our farm was close by'.

Knowledge of the animal kingdom was very limited sixty years ago, there were no nature documentaries from which children could learn the ways of the otter or water dog as it was commonly known. Lack of understanding bred fear in peoples minds to such an extent, that men crossing the canal on their way to Ynynysfach Steel Works, filled their trouser legs with cockle shells. The idea was to fool the otter into thinking it was cracking a bone when all it was doing was crunching a mouthful of cockle shells. There wasn't a word of truth in the old wives tale that an otter held onto a limb until he heard it crack, nevertheless the gruesome story helped safeguard the harmless otters.

The Bridge over the Canal.   Courtesy: Merthyr Public Libraries

As a result, the children kept well away from the water's edge, and spent the afternoon on the canal bank playing leap frog or making daisy chains for each other.

'I always picked a bunch of wild roses to take home, but they used to open and fall apart the next day. They were lovely days back there', Nell said with a far away look in her eyes.

Quite a number of people during those hard times, in order to make extra cash had a shop in the front room where goods could be 'Put on the Book', until pay day. All items purchased had a halfpenny or penny added onto the right price because the shopkeeper had to wait for the money.

'Some shopkeepers fleeced their customers by adding twice as much for having goods on tick, but customers unfortunately were obliged to put up with this sharp practice or go hungry.'

Nell who is partially blind, joined the residential family at Sandbrook House in 1985 and I've yet to see her without a lovely smile expressing a deep contentment for the care she receives at Sandbrook House.

Nell Roberson

Jim Pearce
born 18th November, 1905

Jim was the youngest of five children born to James and Mary Pearce living then in Old Bridge Street, Merthyr. At about the age of six, Jim remembers going to Georgetown School dressed in a shirt his mother had cut out from one discarded by her husband, a pullover she'd knitted herself and a peaked cap fastened down with a button.

'I thought I was king of the castle with my new studded boots, I used to polish them every day when I got home from school ready for the following morning. Boys from poorer families used to wear dabs as five shillings was a lot to pay for boots when money was hard come by'.

One thing Jim never did was take a lunch box to school like the rest of the class. On inquiring why, I received the following reply.

'Rowley Jones let me share his because he was my special friend'.

Apparently Rowley was quite a lad and when Jim and he got together there was nothing too hot or heavy for the pair. One of their favourite pranks was tying the door knobs of two houses together with string then knocking the doors and running away. As both knobs were firmly tied, the doors wouldn't open until someone went along to cut the string. They also by devious ways got into the section of school yard reserved for girls only. Once inside the forbidden compound, Jim and Rowley spent the remainder of break chasing hysterical girls in the hope of stealing a kiss. When someone clecked to the Headmaster, both boys were punished but unfortunately that wasn't the end of the matter. On arriving home Jim's mother boxed his ears and sent him to bed without supper.

Jim Pearce senior who worked in Cyfarthfa Steel Works also had a side line which proved quite profitable. He made wooden replicas of railway engines and sold them for five shillings each. Mr. Pearce knew a man who for a small commission, was willing to take the engines round the other steel companies in Merthyr Borough to sell them to the workers.

'There was no middle class those days', said Jim, 'you were either rich or poor, so when my sister Harriet found a job in Oxford with a well to do family, we though she was the cats whiskers. Girls in service didn't have much pay those days, but beside her board and lodge our Harriet received one pound a week and was able to send five shillings home to help mother'.

Once a year Jim went away to Barry Island in Ernie Shows organ playing charabanc. The trip was paid for by John Morgan the well known founder and organiser of The Ragged School. Only children who attended his Sunday class on a regular basis were able to go to the seaside or join in other events financed by John Morgan. The children took their own lunch but were given a packet of sweets and an apple or orange in case they felt hungry on the way.

Once on the sands Jim would head for the donkeys and spend his penny on a ride along the beach. When the novelty of building sand castles had worn off, he'd be up to his old tricks of chasing the girls for a kiss.

Othertimes he'd hide behind a rock while the girls undressed and steal their clothes but this prank backfired when a lady sitting on the beach saw what he'd been up to and promptly notified the police. Jim spent the rest of the day explaining his behaviour to the Bobby on duty and when finally he left the Police Station it was time to go home.

The following year Jim decided to be a good boy. Leaving the girls to their own devices, he spent the afternoon swimming in the sea. When he came out of the water at the other end of the beach, he couldn't find the spot where he'd left his clothes. The beach was crowded with day trippers so to find his clothes was like looking for a needle in a haystack. A nice kind attendant in the beach hut for Lost Children, gave Jim a towel to cover his lower body. Having removed the soaking swimming trunks, he was completely naked except for the towel and was ribbed unmercifully the entire journey home. His mother was furious with her wayward son when he turned up minus his clothes and after reading him the Riot Act, she gave him a good spanking.

I wish I could find my clothes.

None of the punishments did a thing to change Jim for the better. As a teenager he has vivid recollections of a certain Monday morning when he took his older brother's suit to Harry Pragg's pawn shop.

'Can I borrow three halfpennies 'til next Monday?' he asked Harry.

'I suppose so, but you'll have to pay one half penny interest on the loan so I expect tuppence back.'

All that week Jim was too busy running errands to get into mischief. In the meantime, he was tormented with visions of how his brother would react if he found out.

'I think he'd scalp me first then start asking questions'.

Luckily for Jim the deed was never discovered, although whenever money was urgently needed, the suit could be seen hanging in Harry's window in full view of passers by.

He remembers staying with his Bopa Sal who lived in Cefn Coed and many times when he came down on a Sunday morning, an old lady blue with cold would be sitting in front of the roaring fire warming her hands. She was known as Bess 'Marcus', and spent her time walking the river bank at day break picking fresh watercress. Because Bopa Sal was an old friend and a favoured client of the old lady, Bess would spare two penny worth of cress. It was a tit for tat situation, as Bess Marcus never left the house without a cup of tea flavoured with a drop of the old hard stuff to warm her up.

Jim made friends with the local children and played 'King of the Castle' on Garreg Fawr the huge rock standing on the site where Llysfaen Home is situated. Another game was playing round the lamplight which stood in the centre of Cefn Triangle. Because their houses circled the lamplight, the parents had only to glance through the kitchen window to check whether the children were safe. The lamplighter had two different caps. When he went round lighting the lamps, he wore a brown tweed cap. This was changed for one of black serge when carrying out his official duty of the School Absentee Officer. Cefn children who mitched classes, lived in dread of him finding out and paying a viist to their homes.

The lamplighter, Cefn Coed. He was also the truant officer.

'The Bobby Greencoat was forever knocking at our door. I must have been one of the biggest mitchers in the school', laughed Jim.

Jim also has a vivid memory of attending the funeral of a man known in Cefn as Rhys Ffrmwr who had been a big butty of his Uncle Ieuan.

'Bopa was dressed in severe black and Uncle Ieuan, one of the bearers, wore his funeral suit. Rhys Thomas lived in The Triangle and we had a job to get into the house because of the crowds gathered there. I'd heard the expression 'Black with people', used to describe a crowd, but on this particular occasion it happened to be true. When we went into the house, a little girl about my own age took our coats. I recognised her from playing on The Twyn. Her name was Doris but I didn't know it was her father we'd come to pay our respects to. The body was taken to the cemetery in a horse drawn hearse and for the first time I saw white feathered plumes on the horses heads. The miners began singing a sad hymn and the crowd joined in. I asked Doris what the hymn was called'.

'Cwm Rhondda', she replied and burst out crying. 'I haven't got a Daddy anymore', she sobbed.

'With that I started to cry myself. When we went back to the house for tea and sandwiches, Doris and her brother were sitting at their mother's knee all crying together. That was the last funeral I went to until I grew up and was able to listen without crying like a big girl'.

Despite his love for the girls, Jim remained a bachelor. In 1988 he became too ill to look after himself and joined the residents at Sandbrook House which is now his permanent home.

Jim Pearce

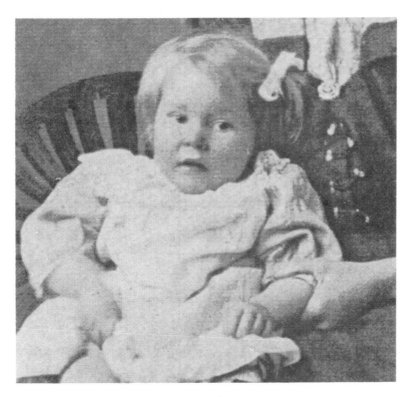

May Williams
born 2nd November, 1903

May was one of two surviving children from a family of four. They weren't well off by a long way but her father made sufficient in his job as timber miner in Gethin Pit, Abercanaid to make ends meet. As the children grew up more money for food and clothing was essential so May's Dad left the pit to work in the Furnaces at Dowlais Steel Works. On pay day, the children used to wait by the garden gate for their father to come home. He always brought a Fry's coconut bar for each of them and flowers from his friend's allotment for their mother.

'I learned to speak Welsh pretty well in Brecon Road Infant School but find it difficult to recall what kind of toys we played with except for the sand boxes and sticks of modelling clay. As an infant, I was given a small wooden box half filled with sand damped enough to trace patterns or objects with my finger. I also liked making dolls and animals out of clay because it felt lovely and soft in my hands. A small piece of clay rolled into a ball formed the head, a bigger ball became the body and four pieces were moulded into arms and legs. Next, part of the head was covered with yellow clay for hair, a bit of red for a mouth, and two spots of blue for eyes. The hardest part was fixing the parts together as they kept falling off'.

When May moved to the Junior School, she remembers doing classroom drill twice a week with her clothes tucked inside knee length navy bloomers which sported a pocket on one leg for keeping a handkerchief. It wasn't really the easiest place to retrieve a handkerchief from in an emergency but nobody seemed to mind the inconvenience.

Miss Harris would stand in front of the class calling out instructions to the pupils;

'Legs apart girls, arms to the side, heads up, breath in, now follow me'.

'You'd think it was an elephant stampede by the noise we made swinging our arms in and out and jumping up and down on the wooden planks. On very cold days, we'd be sweating pints after classroom drill and would blow down our blouse fronts to cool off.'

At home, Mary made long tube like lengths of corkwork which were sewn onto pieces of hard cardboard the size and shape of her feet to make colourful bedroom slippers. Or she'd knit squares of different coloured wools and when there were sufficient, crochet them together to make a bed cover.

From a child she was absolutely fascinated by water maybe because the Taff flowed past the back garden and nothing thrilled her more than to cross and recross the river at a certain shallow spot known by the locals to be quite safe for paddling across to the other side. Sometimes her clothes got wet and when this happened her mother would be very cross and May would be sent to bed without supper.

About this time May's five year old brother called Haydn David fell down the steps by the Grawen Public House and hit the front of his head causing severe brain damage which proved fatal. May remembers the little coffin covered with masses of wild flowers picked by his playmates and wreaths hanging on the handles covering the top of the hearse all the way to Cefn Cemetery followed by their relatives and most of the inhabitants of Brecon Road.

People not able to buy food could apply for the 'Parish', which took a great deal of courage as the men investigating the case, beside being rude wanted to know the ins and outs of a cat's behind before parting with a few shillings.

'You'd think they were paying the money from their own pockets', was a favourite expression from those who'd been before the board.

On asking May if her parents had been obliged to ask the parish for help she gave me the following reply.

'Father had a big kidney and wouldn't ask for help if we were starving, and mother was just as bad. They didn't believe in credit so it was a case of - if we couldn't afford it we did without'

Something that impressed May was the way women over thirty seemed to grow old overnight and remain like that until they expired. She can't remember her mother or grandmother ever being what you'd call young or middle aged.

'It must have been due to the way they dressed in severe black, the only bit of colour worn by my mother was a floral pinafore and even that had a deep black border'.

The black lead iron grate. *Courtesy: Gweno Hugh Jones*

'One of my chores at home was cleaning the brass candlesticks on the mantle piece and the brass rail underneath but I was never asked to black lead the iron grate. Mother would almost kill herself in an effort to keep it clean and shiny, her hands used to shine like a blackie's for hours after she'd finished with the blacking. Our hearth of square flagstones had to be white-stoned each day, otherwise it would be impossible to keep it looking nice, the way mother liked to see it. She was terribly house proud and very fussy about keeping things tidy.'

Courtesy: Greater London Council Photographic Collection.
Learning how to blacklead a grate and to lay a fire, Dulwich Hamlet School, 1907.

May was an industrious little girl making clothes out of material scraps for her dolls and darning socks in the dim gas light. She was bewitched when the gas mantle would begin to burn out.

'It would flicker and turn lovely shades of red and blue. Suddenly when you least expected, it would blacken all over and crumble to bits.'

Most children liked to receive chocolate or games for presents but May preferred a new blouse to go with her gymslip or new underclothes.

There was a nice garden at the back of their house where May had her own little plot for growing gilly flowers and Lilies of the Valley. Her father grew rhubarb and planted redcurrant, blackcurrant and gooseberry bushes so there was plenty of fruit for making turnovers and tarts. Occasionally they had rabbit pie and her mother used to make a hole in the top pastry for the steam to escape from a china funnel placed underneath.

May went to Tabernacle Chapel, Brecon Road where they held soires twice or three times a year. The vestry tables would be laiden with blanchmanges, jellies trifles, blackberry, apple and gooseberry tarts and jugs of ideal milk. Lemonade was the favourite drink but at the end of the evening everybody finished up with a mug of Rowntree's cocoa. There was great excitement at Tabernacle Church when a new minister called Arthur Davies arrived, not only was he smart and good looking but unattached.

'We went to chapel three times on Sunday and attended weekly meetings in the hope he'd fancy one of us. Never before had the old members seen so many smart or fashionably dressed young girls at every congregational meeting. Much to our dismay he wasn't in the least impressed by our finery and after receiving a call to Porthcawl, married a plain mousy girl who you wouldn't look at once let alone twice.'

Having reached the age of eighty nine and finding it difficult to look after herself, May was obliged this year to join the family at Sandbrook House. She is very happy with her new friends and glad to be surrounded with a staff of caring helpers.

May Williams

Georgina Carpenter
born 18th July, 1911

Georgina was named after her mother but her brother and three sisters decided on a shorter version, so from that day onward she became Gina to family and friends alike.

Gina remembers quite clearly the first day she was taken to the Infants' Class at Dowlais Central School.

'When I saw my mother leaving, I screamed and screamed to go home, but she took no notice. The teacher locked the classroom door to prevent me running away and said I was a naughty little girl for upsetting the other children. Every morning I threw a tantrum and carried on something awful in the hope that Mam would relent, but it didn't work. Daddy said it was early days and given time I'd grow to like school. For once he was wrong'.

Grandmother Isabella used to make white pinafores with a frill round the neck for Gina, to which her mother pinned a clean handkerchief each morning before tying back the long fair hair with blue ribbon. When the bell rang at dinner time, Gina, who was now in the Junior School, collected her small sister Iris and hand in hand they ran home for lunch. A basin of piping hot potato or split pea soup would be ready on the table when they arrived but only on rare occasions would the soup contain meat.

Teatime was again a basic meal of buttered bread spread with treacle or home made jam except on special occasions when suet pudding sweetened with syrup was served.

'My brother liked 'Spotted Dick' because it was loaded with currants and raisins', said Gina, 'but my favourite was apple dumpling and thick custard.'

The three puddings mentioned above, after being prepared were wrapped in a white pleated cloth to allow the suet to swell then placed in a saucepan on the open fire. When done the pudding swelled up to thrice its original size filling the black iron saucepan.

The 1914 War ended when Gina was seven. She recalls standing with all the family at Pant Cenotaph listening to her father play the last post on his silver bugle. This was the second ceremony the family attended in a matter of weeks, the first occasion being the presentation of the silver bugle. How proud Gina felt when she saw the crowd gathered on the Town Hall steps waiting for a famous army Colonel to present her father with his silver bugle.

Saturday was market day in Dowlais and the children were up early to go shopping with their mother. There was a farmer's stall selling fresh eggs, salted butter and Caerphilly cheese. Other stalls sold galvanised buckets, bathpans, bowls, sweeping and scrubbing brushes. Almost anything one needed for the home was there on display.

'When Mam finished shopping she'd give us a penny each to spend at Davies the Rock Shop, and I'd buy a bag of multi colour sweet fishes which lasted for ever if you sucked them slowly.'

Mr. S.O. Davies the Miners' Agent, lived in 'Gwent House', Mount Pleasant, Dowlais and when Gina was about ten year old, she recalls hearing men outside their house calling her father dreadful names. It was 1921 the year of the pit strike and the men were bent on preventing Gina's father who was a blacksmith underground, from going to work.

'They threw stones at the windows and tried to force the door, we were terrified but someone fetched Mr. S.O. Davies. After talking

PARISH of ABERCYNON; BAND of HOPE "THE FAIRY RING" DEC 29th 1921.

Courtesy: Bill Jones. Welsh Industrial & Maritime Museum Cardiff

with the angry men for a few minutes, they calmed down and walked quietly away. Thank goodness the miners respected Mr. Davies, otherwise I shudder to think what the outcome would have been'.

Alfonso Street, Dowlais was so named because it overflowed with Spanish families who came over from Spain to work in the Ivor Works. Gina formed a friendship with a Adela Iturrate who was born after her parents settled in Dowlais. As a result she spoke both languages and taught Gina quite a lot of Spanish.

Mr. J.R. Davies the headmaster of Dowlais School was also Superintendant of Ivor English Congregational Chapel where Gina attended Sunday School. Every Sunday evening, Grandma Isabella called at 5.30pm to take Gina and Iris to evening service. But the girls preferred Monday because it was Band of Hope night and instead of mournful hymns they sat in a circle listening to Bible stories and sang children's songs.

Tragedy struck in the shape of the dreadful diphtheria when Gina was ten years old. The hospitals were choc a block with children near to death but although hospitals offered the best hope of survival, Gina's mother refused to let the doctor take her daughter there. Instead, she nursed the child at home despite the risk to her other children. Miraculously not one of them was infected and Gina made a complete recovery. An aunt keeping a farm in Brecon, took the frail sickly girl to stay with her for six weeks and when Gina returned home she was strong as a Welsh mountain pony and fit enough to go back to school. At eleven years of age, Gina tried the Scholarship Exam and passed to go to Cyfarthfa Grammar School.

'At long last I was leaving Dowlais Central for good', she laughed.

When it was time to choose a career, Gina decided to become a fever nurse but having left the grammar school at seventeen there was a year to wait before she could be accepted in the Mardy Isolation Hospital.

'No way was I going to wait a whole year', said Gina, 'so I cheated my age by telling the Matron I was eighteen. I did three years at the Mardy and a further two and half years training at the General Hospital. I must tell you this funny story that happened during my training in the Mardy.'

'We had a talking parrot on my ward which beside keeping children amused seemed to be a great favourite until little Horace from Treharris was admitted. He didn't like Percy at all and one afternoon we discovered to our horror that they were both missing. A thorough search of the grounds was carried out but Horace and the parrot were nowhere to be found. Taking a bedpan to the sluice, I was petrified to hear blood curdling screams coming from the lavatory. Pushing the door, I was just in time to prevent Horace flushing the parrot down the water closet. Percy was never the same after his very traumatic experience, and became agitated at the least sound or sudden movement. Soon afterwards, Matron told us a spinster friend offered to take Percy home to her cottage in the country. A few weeks later, Matron received a letter saying, Percy had settled down beautifully in his new surroundings and was a marvellous companion'.

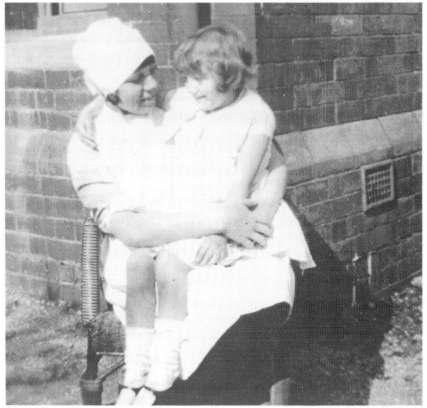

Gina with one of her patients.

Gina can remember clearly the kind of meals served on the childrens ward.

Breakfast consisted of cremated toast or porridge stiff enough to paste wallpaper. Lunch was mainly a vegetable dish except on Wednesday when they had stewed rabbit. Tea was the customary meal served in every hospital throughout the country, i.e. bread and strawberry jam. Years after Gina finished nursing, on seeing anyone eating bread spread with butter and jam, she'd remark;

'I see you're having hospital tea'.

When visitors brought fruit, it was taken to the kitchen, cut into pieces and shared out among those less fortunate. The same applied if someone made a cake for their little girl or boy, every child in the ward received a sliver however small.

A dish called 'Soup', was served at suppertime but it was in reality gravy with potatoes left over from lunch, this was always served hot owing to the gravy turning lumpy when it cooled. Before being settled for the night, the children were given an enamel mug of cocoa which was the general drink with every meal.

Every patient had to drink a medicine made from licorice and called Black Jack on Saturday morning or half a cup of Senna. The idea was to flush their bowels open and nurse stood over each one until the last drop was consummed. Some of the old fashioned remedies we used for curing illnesses are still used today by the older generation. For example, elderberry tea or oil of eucalyptus rubbed back and front and over the soles of the feet is said to cure colds. Fresh pineapple juice gets rid of whooping cough and goose-grease is a sure cure for sore throats.

Two years ago, Gina suffered a stroke on her left side and was taken to the Mardy Hospital where she'd trained many years ago. From there she was transferred to Sandbrook House where the treatment she needed could be administered. Gina is very happy in her new home and grateful to both Officer and staff for their kindness and constant care.

Georgina Carpenter

Reg Morgan
born 3rd January, 1910

Reg was one of five children born to Edith and Price Morgan.

One of his first memories centres around Caedraw School, where so many of his schoolmates came to grief on the outside iron staircase. Although warned of the danger the vertical flight was a constant challenge to the most foolhardy who when dared, swung like half pint Tarzans from the open rungs. A serious fall more times than not resulted in the victim's limbs being encased in unsightly leg irons which were difficult to manoeuvre and heavy to drag along.

On arriving at school, the children formed lines in the school yard then marched off one behind the other into their own classroom. Mr. Jones their headmaster was also music conductor for the Dowlais and Penydarren Choir. There were several women teachers on the staff who were as radical as the masters when it came to applying the cane. The Infant School consisted of one large room equipped with play things to keep the children occupied, the rest of the building formed the Junior School.

When Reg moved from infant to junior school he was thrilled to share a double desk with another boy. There was a ledge running the length of the desk to hold pencils, rubbers and rulers, there was also a china inkwell on either side of the desk and a pen with a scratchy nib for each pupil. The inkwells when empty were refilled with black tacky ink which was kept in a brown earthenware jar with - INK - written in large capitals.

Most days Reg went home dinner time but if he was lucky enough to own a penny he could buy a basin of broth from the school kitchen.

'The broth was all right', said Reg, 'but if I had a penny off my mother for being good, I'd rather buy 2 toffee apples from a lady in Clare Street who sold them to the children for a halfpenny each'.

The boys played football during break which usually ended in a free for all fight followed by a couple of 'Benders', from Mr. Jones. The older boys put exercise books in their pants to soften the blow but Mr. Jones wasn't that stupid and added an extra bender for deception. Many of his friends mitched school without their parents being aware of the fact. They'd leave home in the morning as if going to school then go fishing or play in the woods until they heard the school bell ring at home time.

After the boys had played truant for a number of weeks, Mr. Jones would contact the Bobby Greencoat to report their absence from class, and Miss Gladys Lewis would call at the home of each absentee to see what was wrong. The parents were usually stunned to hear what their son had been up to and a good thrashing with dad's leather belt was a sure guarantee it wouldn't happen again.

The Inky wasn't far from where Reg lived and when the blackberries were ripe, the brambles along the incline would be laden with juicy berries.

'My mother used to make a big circle of pastry and bake it on the Llywen which is the welsh name for a bakestone. When the pastry was done, she'd spread the blackberries on top and let them cook for a few minutes. Before eating the blackberry turnover, my job was to sprinkle it with sugar and put a lump of butter in the middle, it was really scrumptious. Sometimes I picked more blackberries than were needed, and I sold whatever Mother didn't want for a few coppers to our neighbours, this being one method of getting enough money to go

The Soup Kitchen.

to the flicks on Saturday afternoon.'

Being prone to colds and a sore throat was one of the reasons why Reg dreaded the long endless wintery months when his throat was smeared with thick smelly goose grease and swathed in a piece of his father's flannel shirt.

'You could smell me coming a mile away, even Billy my best friend refused to sit next to me and I was ostracised by the gang until my throat got better'.

At seven, Reg became a choir boy in the Parish Church and the family went along to admire his ruff and gleaming white surplic.

'He looked like a little angel', his mother was heard to remark while having a cuppa with their next door neighbour.

But neither the choir master or verger shared her opinion when they found a couple of goldfish swimming in the font water during a christening the following Sunday.

'Riggsy the Verger, laid the finest clout on my head I'd ever had the misfortune to experience and Musical Watkins not to be outdone, cornered me in the cloistures after choir practice and boxed both my ears'.

During the 1921 Miners Strike, Caedraw School was turned into a soup kitchen. Children whose fathers were out on strike were entitled to free soup and a chunk of bread at their school soup kitchen. Every lunch time a long queue of youngsters carrying spoons and basins would be lined up outside the school gates waiting eagerly for their turn to go in.

When he was twelve, Reg moved up to form five or scholarship class from which you either went to the Intermediate School, or were sent to one of the senior schools. Unfortunately Reg failed the exam and was transfered to Abermorlais Senior. At fourteen, he tried the scholarship exam for the second time and passed with flying colours. He went on to become the Headmaster of Highwood Hospital School, Brentford, Essex.

The following lines were written by Reg Morgan.

In the Service of Youth

Education has taken grips on pre-education followed by modern equipment in Infant method. Young children were keen to follow a new type of learning called the Comprehensive Plan to which Grammar and Technical schools quickly conformed.

The 'scholarship', so many including myself had fought hard to attain and considered a great achievement when successful, was cancelled out. No longer were exam failures transferred to Senior Schools until the leaving age of fourteen. The Comprehensive Plan had certainly taken over.

'A lot of water has passed under the bridge since those days', Reg said with a sad smile, 'but it's nice to have memories to look back on, even sad ones are better than none at all'.

After both his mother and his wife died, Reg was lonely and decided to find a home where he'd have care and companionship. For that reason he became a resident at Sandbrook House and has never regretted his wise decision.

Reg Morgan

Group members relaxing after a workshop in Sandbrook House.

Staff of Sandbrook House.

Some members of the workshop waiting for their 'cuppa'.

Tegfan House,
Trecynnon, Aberdare

With side view of old Workhouse at extreme right.   Courtesy: Meirion Davies

The old Tegfan Workhouse which is now a day centre.   Courtesy: Meirion Davies

Tegfan

Tegfan Home for the Elderly, dates back to the early 19th century and was built as an Infirmary in 1871, by the Merthyr Tydfil Union Board of Guardians. Six years later in 1877, it was converted into an Industrial School for pauper children with the sole purpose of training them to become tailors, shoemakers etc. Being dressed alike, the children were easily recognised, as they marched through Aberdare town to Aberaman House for their annual treat. In 1895, it was decided to discard the pauper uniforms, during which year, no less than 124 children were being cared for and taught a trade.

Up until then, elementary education was confined to whatever was taught within the four walls of the Industrial School but 1910 brought a much needed change. The paupers were permitted to attend elementary schools where they could integrate with valley children from Aberdare and the surrounding district.

Cottage Homes were set up in Llwycoed, Cwmbach, Hirwaun and Abercwmboi where foster parents were encouraged to create a real family atmosphere. Gradually, the stigma of pauperism disappeared once and for all time.

The number of children being cared for between 1910-1914 was recorded in Kelly's Directories of South Wales as 200 but there is no mention of the Industrial School by 1918-1919.

During the Great War, the School was also used as a temporary military hospital for our Dominion Troops and that may possibly be the reason for any ommission in Kelly's directories. During the Great War, many wounded soldiers recovering in the hospital, wrote verses, words of appreciation or just signed their names in an autograph book. Some examples have been included on the page following this brief history of Tegfan.

In 1929 the same establishment became known as 'Windsor House Poor Law Institiution', more commonly referred to by local inhabitants as Aberdare Workhouse. A thorough face lift took place in 1930 when the Workhouse was transferred from the Merthyr Union to Glamorgan County Council. Facilities were made available for alterations, additions, redecorating, electrical rewiring plus the installation of a new lift.

From 1949 the name was changed to 'Tegfan Hostel', a home for aged male patients. On September 2nd, 1961 a grand 'Open Day' took place where any visitor could inspect bright hotel style bedrooms, tastefully decorated lounges, halls and dining rooms. Tegfan grounds were packed with guests and Aberdare people who prior to patronising sideshows and stalls, were eager to chat with members of the 170 elderly men residing at the Home.

Llwydcoed Silver Band, played throughout the afternoon while visitors enjoyed refreshments and a welcome cup of tea in brilliant sunshine.

A modernisation scheme for Tegfan Hostel, costing £45,000 was on the agenda in 1965, a complete change of policy was about to take place in which the total of 170 residents would be reduced to 130. For the first time in the history of the establishment, 68 women as well as 62 men would be accomodated at Tegfan Hostel. The first female, with the exception of the staff or visitors, to move into the New Block, was Mrs. Martha Watkins.

When introduced to Mr. Maldwyn Howells the warden, Martha recognised him as the boy who once lived next door to her at Engineers Row, Abernant. Two other ladies namely Miss Gwen Williams of Penywaun and Mrs. Hannah Williams of Herbert Street, Aberdare, joined Mrs. Watkins to be counted among the first residents. From an estimated list of 300 individuals, waiting to be admitted to Homes for the Aged when a vacancy occured, three more ladies entered Tegfan the following week.

The opening of Tegfan on the 13th October, 1992   *Courtesy: Cynon Valley Library, Aberdare*

The number of male staff was reduced so extra female helpers could be appointed in order to cope with the new set up, also, the residents were given every opportunity to lead a full social life if they so wished.

Over two decades later 'Tegfan Resource Centre for the Elderly', was completed with an official opening ceremony on October 13th, 1992. Words do little to describe the outer appearance of the complex or the superb interior furnishings and decoration. To put it in a nutshell, except for a very special ingredient, Tegfan could easily be mistaken for a first class hotel. You may have guessed already what that special ingredient is. Yes, an inexplicable aura of deep contentment that only comes when one is surrounded by those who truly care about those in their charge.

The above history of Tegfan, has been pieced together from documents kindly loaned me by the Cynon Valley Library, Aberdare, for which I am extremely grateful. Thank you Sarah and Alice for your cooperation.

Iris Roderick Thomas
14th April, 1993

These pages have been kindly loaned by Cynon Valley Libraries Aberdare

When Writing in Albums, Memory enures.
With the Greatest Pleasure, I write in yours.
When the Words of this Verse, are linn on this Page
And the leaves of this Book, are Yellow with Age.
Then think of Me, kindly, and Don't forget.
That Wherever I am, I Remember You yet.

Corporal E.J. Taylor, one of the First Landing
Heroic in the Dardanelles. April 25th 1915.
1st The Lancashire Fusiliers 29th Division. 12/2/17.

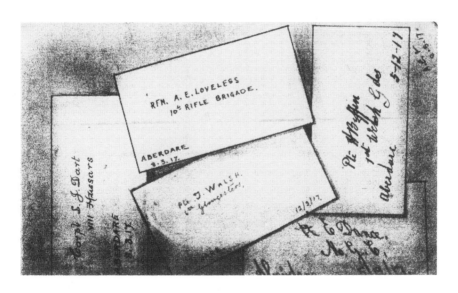

*Pages from an autograph book from the time when Tegfan became a Military Hospital
for our Dominion Troops 1914-1918.*

Mary Edith Davies
born 3rd January, 1893
100 Year Celebration

Mary Edith Davies known to both family and friends as Nan, was born on 3rd January 1893 in Mostyn, North Wales, where her family still reside.

Nan went into service and trained as a Nanny in London. She worked for several families during an era when the expression, 'Upstairs' or 'Below Stairs', summed up a person's position. The families, including doctors and many professional people, have never forgotten the way Nan looked after them. Each Christmas, cards and gifts from all over the globe arrive at Tegfan, in appreciation for her years of faithful service.

William Davies, Nan's late husband, was a commercial traveller who met Nan when he was working in London. They got engaged and planned like all young people in love, to marry at the earliest opportunity, but it was not to be. The lady of the house where Nan was employed, died shortly after her fourth child was born and her devastated husband begged Nan to stay on and bring up the children. Putting aside her personal plans, Nan showed a true spirit of unselfish dedication to others, by concentrating on rearing the four children. She was 48 years old by the time her responsibilities were fulfilled and she was free to marry William.

The couple set up house at Windsor Street, Trecynon, Aberdare, where they made many friends and were blissfully happy to be together at last. Unfortunately, Nan was widowed 20 years ago and lived alone until at 94 years of age, she fell and broke her hip. She was admitted to hospital for treatment, and on 17th March 1986, she was transferred to Tegfan.

When Tegfan closed in 1988, Nan was transferred to Troedyrhiw House, but was fortunate to be one of the first residents to return to Tegfan when it was re-opened in 1992.

Nan, is a very 'regal' lady. Popular with both staff and family at the Home. Her great friend is Esther Lewis who also resides at Tegfan. Their friendship blossomed from their very first encounter and Esther, who is extremely protective of her friend's interests, has been a great comfort and support since Nan's sight sadly deteriorated.

The family of William Davies, Nan's late husband, are most supportive, especially Mrs. Thelma Drew and Mrs. Menna Price, who spend time with Nan almost every day.

It's lovely to see for oneself, the attention and consideration given to Nan by both family and the entire staff at Tegfan Resource Centre for the Elderly.

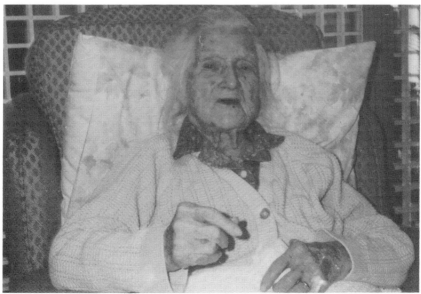

Our Nan.

Albert Charles Williams
born 31st August, 1907

Albert, his two brothers and only sister were born in the Gadlys Aberdare, which is a stone throw from the pit, and the County School. Their father Tom Williams, was an ordinary council worker, earning small money. There were no wide smooth tarmac roads like we have today, only rough narrow uneven cart tracks. The time had arrived for decent roads to replace the old cart tracks, and Tom had the back breaking task of hauling the stones from the quarry for progress to begin. Only well to do people could afford a horse and trap, so walking was the main mode of transport from village to village.

'Stony lanes were rough cart tracks, played havoc with our feet, and as a child, mine were always cut and bleeding, from a long dusty walk into Aberaman or Cwmbach', said Albert. 'Children today don't know they are born. In our day, if we wanted to go anywhere, we had to get there under our own stream, using 'Shanks's Pony'. Today cars take them to and from school, cars take them shopping, they even get in the car to call on a neighbour in the same street. No wonder the world is in the state it is, people are gone mad.'

Every morning at five, Albert was awakened by the pit hooter wailing loud enough to wake the dead. Turning over, he'd go back to sleep until his mother called the children for breakfast. Except for the early morning alert, the pit hooter would only blow to warn the neighbourhood of an accident at the mine. When this happened, people from all over Aberdare, would gather at the pit head. Almost everybody living in the vicinity had at least one family member working underground.

'First down would be the rescue team', said Albert, 'perhaps after long hours of waiting, a stretcher with a dead or injured miner would be brought to the surface. Volunteers carried the stretchers, through a maze of streets, all the way to the hospital. Weeping wives and mothers not knowing whether their own husband, father, or son had been spared, following behind. Prayers were said at the pit head by local ministers, and everyone knelt when called on to repeat the Lord's Prayer'.

When school broke up for the Summer holidays, armed with a pen knife, some old sacking, a bottle of water, and a doorstep of bread spread with thick dripping. Albert was equipped to face the most vicious of foes waiting to challenge him, at the top of the Griag. After making a frame from some branches, he would drape the sacking around to form a tent. This rough shelter, protected him not only from wind and rain, but was a place of refuge from wild lions and tigers on the prowl.

Each day at early morn, the little lad could be seen climbing up the steep slope of the Graig, and every morning at dusk he'd be seen on the downward track. When the whimberries ripened, Albert would spend hours on his hands and knees picking the fruit. At the end of the day, he'd be covered with scratches from the picky undergrowth, while his hands were stained purple from whimberry juice. His mother preserved most of the fruit, and made tarts from the whimberries left over. Some Summers there was a glut of whimberries on the Graig, and Albert picked far too much fruit for his mother's need.

'I'd sell to people living in the Gadlys, and put every penny in my money-box. At the end of the Summer when the brambles were black with berries, I'd spend hours collecting blackberries. I made a lot of money selling to our neighbours and my money box was soon full. It was worthwhile when I saw the blackberry turnover bubbling on the bakestone, and I quickly forgot how painful the scratches were as my teeth sank into a large slice of delicious turnover'.

Sometimes, Albert helped to plant potatoes or erect bean sticks in his father's allotment on the ground where Cwmdare Technical College now stands. His father built a shed from zincs and old planks for storing tools and manure. When his work in the allotments was finished, Albert's dad, would rock to and fro in a wobbly rocking chair he kept in the shed, old Dai the collie would lay with one eye open, at his master's feet, guarding him with his life.

'Wherever my father was, you'd find Dai, no-one could have a more faithful friend than old Dai, the whole family went into mourning on the day he died'.

A Special Event was held each year at Aberdare Park, where Albert's father being such a keen gardener, spent most of the afternoon in the flower and vegetable marquee. Some dahlias grown by local gardeners were as good as any grown by London experts, but it was the outsized onion sets, giant leeks, and evenly matched turnips that held his interest.

The big parade headed by the Salvation Army Band, began its circuit to Aberdare Park round about noon. Cheering crowds lined the streets to see jazz bands, flower decked carts with girls in fancy dress, shire horses, St. Johns Ambulance Cadets, Boy Scouts and handcuffed men pretending to be the chain gang, go marching past. Inside the park a large circle was roped off where jazz bands went through their figures. The best fancy dress costumes were also judged in this ring as well as Shire horses.

'There were always a dozen or more jazz bands from different valleys waiting to take part in the competition. Every band played their own signature tune on the kazoos and had the name of their jazz band on the big drum. Red Indians, Blackies, Hebrew Slaves, Mexicans turned out in full force, and there was always a Jazz Band dressed in Miners clothes complete with lamps and picks', explained Albert.

Rescue teams from underground gave first aid demonstrations, Boy Scouts showed how to light fires and tie knots. Superb Shire horses displaying their winning rosettes, were paraded round the grounds by proud owners. After the horse parade, Albert always met up with his father in the tent where canaries and bullfinches were due to be judged, but the biggest thrill of all was finding out whether Dai, their own collie, had landed a prize in the dog show.

Another enjoyable day was spent at the Eisteddfod Abernant Park, where adult and childrens' choirs competed for top awards, to take back to their own valley.

'I wasn't keen on the annual church treat held in the hospital

Aberdare Carnival - Decorated car with Troupe of Pierrots.

A Post-War Jazz Band
  Back Row: Lennie Jones, Mattie Williams, Mr. Wallman, Mavis Sears, Mrs. Whately, 'Jonesy',
Margaret John, Billy Hunt, -, Vincent Thomas, Mr. & Mrs Joe Hunt, Lily Sears, Vernon Lewis,
  Beryl Mahoney, The Author, Ira Hunt, Mrs. Leonard, Kath Murphy, Miss Hunt.

grounds', said Albert, 'but as the food was free, it was stupid to stay at home. I tell you another thing. When I started work as an errand boy, in the grocer shop owned by Wm. Harris, I did all the deliveries on Shanks Pony for just a few bob weekly. Although the shop owned two horses and carts, the drivers would never dream of stopping to give me a ride even if I was on my last legs. Yes, shopkeepers made boys work for their money back in the days when cooked ham was 2/6 a lb and Brook Bond tea was 7 pennies a quarter pound. If you had a quid then, you thought you were a millionaire.'

Ted (Kid) Lewis   *Jimmy Wilde*

Albert told about walking from Aberdare to Mountain Ash and back just for the fun of it, or over to Merthyr to see Cuthbert Taylor sparring in the boxing promotions held in a marquee behind Ernie Snows Garage.

'I was boxing mad at the time and remember going over the mountain again to see Tommy Farr box at Merthyr Drill Hall. Another time I caught the train to Cardiff to see Jack Peterson at Greyfriars Hall, win hands down. Why a professional doctor wanted to box, is something hard to imagine. Perhaps his decision had something to do with his father owning the gymnasium at Cardiff. Jack Francis was the boxing promoter for bouts held in Ynys Field Aberaman, Aberdare and I'll never forget the night, when Dick Diamond slayed his opponent in the first few rounds. We sang ourselves hoarse that night in the local. They were good old days'.

Courtesy: Carolyn Jacob

Jake Kilrain

Tommy Farr

Albert is a grand fellow, always smiling and ready to fall in with whatever's going on at Tegfan. On the first day of five memory packed workshops, Albert apologised for not saying much.

'I can't remember as far back as my childhood, so you'll have to excuse me not joining in like the others', he whispered, as I was preparing to leave.

During the following weeks, Albert became so talkative, that I had my work cut out trying to keep him quiet.

Albert Charles Williams

Eva Augusta Powell
born 5th November, 1903

Eva lived in Wallasey, Cheshire for the first four years of her life until her parents decided to move into the Cynon Valley, Wales. At that time they were a family of three children, Phil, Eva and Vera as Hilda didn't arrive until they were comfortably settled in Cwmaman.

'Before coming to Wales, I can remember my mother taking us to the seaside, I couldn't have been more than four at the time, so I forget the name of the place. Perhaps it was Liverpool, don't write it down because by next week I may discover it was Barry or Swansea. What I do remember as clear as day, is wearing a dress with a sailor collar and a wide brim straw hat. My brother and sister wore sailor suits and straw hats with long ribbon streamers at the back. Although it was the middle of Summer and very hot, we weren't allowed to take any of our clothes off. I wanted to tuck my petticoat into my bloomers like some other children searching for crabs in the rock pools, but Mammy stopped me. We each kept our hats on in case of catching sunstroke but it was hard to enjoy ourselves when dressed in our Sunday best.

Eva talked about the seaside shops, with their rows of tin buckets and wooden spades dangling outside. The tin buckets were real eye catchers with ships or seaside scenes painted in bright colours. Before going to the beach, the children were given three or sixpence to choose whichever bucket they fancied. While Eva, Vera and Phil, were still deciding what to buy, their mother went looking for humbug rock and a tiny momento to add to her collection.

Phil had spent hours at home, making a kite, for their day at the seaside. Using two sticks, a sheet of strong brown packing paper and a roll of string, the boy had made a fine looking kite. Eva and Vera were responsible for cutting and fixing chunks of folded newspaper on the string tail.

'We ran across the beach dragging the kite behind us until a thermal lifted it into the air. Phil made it loop the loop high above our heads by letting the string off the ball but once the wind died down the kite dropped to earth.'

When the children got hungry, they sat on towels and ate salmon paste sandwiches washed down by small beer from pop alley bottles. Refreshed and fed, they played sand castles and touch until it was time to catch the train for home.

During another day trip to the seaside, the children were taken aboard a fishing boat to watch the fish being caught and later sorted out into big barrels.

'I was fascinated', said Eva, 'and when a fisherman gave me his rod to hold, I made up my mind that one day I'd catch fish'.

Eva never forgot the thrill of holding a rod, and years later became an angler herself. In 1944 her son Jackie pushed her in a wheelchair to a stretch of the River Taff where some good size trout had been sighted. Not long after casting in, Eva landed a 9lb 7oz fish. A local paper soon got hold of the story. That evening, a photograph of Eva sitting in her wheelchair, holding the 9lb 7oz trout, was front page news.

'When we moved to Cwmaman. I was five and suffering from asthma. Some attacks were severe, so I was away from school half the time. Up till then my teeth hadn't bothered me because I wasn't allowed to eat sweets but one night I woke with ramping toothache. The pain has disappeared by the time I got up and as my asthma wasn't too bad that day, Mam said I could go to school. Half way through the morning, my tooth began to ache like mad and Miss Boxall said, 'It's got to come out.' Putting her coat on she marched me down the road to the clinic. This was my first visit to clinic and when the dentist came out of the surgery in his white coat, I was petrified. But a funny thing happened that moment making me forget my fright'.

'Are you the little girl's mother?', inquired the dentist.

'Miss Boxall nearly collapsed with embarrassment.'

'I am not married, Sir', she replied blushing.

'That's nothing to do with me, I only want to know about your little girl', the dentist snapped out.

'Everyone in the clinic stopped talking, imagining that I was Miss Boxall's illegitimate child which was a terrible disgrace in those days. My poor teacher was scarlet with temper as the dentist giving her a look of contempt led me into the surgery and closed the door. If he'd pulled every tooth from my mouth without cocaine, I couldn't have cared less. All I wanted, was to get back to school to tell my friends what happened in the clinic. Thankfully the dentist couldn't read my thoughts and took the tooth out under gas, which was painless, though I felt a bit sick on coming round.'

The family lived in a three bedroomed terraced house with slated roof, rafter ceilings, and a back garden large enough to keep chickens, Karki Campbell and Aylesbury ducks. The eggs were collected each day and when the chickens and ducks failed to lay, they were sold as boilers.

The downstairs was quite roomy with a parlour, kitchen, living room and an outside lavatory at the bottom of the garden. The children had a weekly scrub down in a tin bath placed in front of a roaring fire.

'Mam warmed a towel to wrap round me as I got out of the bath and I sat on the stool waiting my turn to be rubbed dry. Nothing can compare with washing in a bath of lovely hot water in front of the fire, however posh the bathroom happens to be'.

About three weeks prior to Christmas, Eva helped prepare fruit puddings that were mixed in a massive earthenware pan, kept specially for this annual occasion. The puddings were boiled on the kitchen fire in Gran's iron boiler but the six 2lb yeast cakes were taken to the corner bakehouse to make sure they were cooked through.

Before emptying the pudding mixture into enamel basins, a dozen three and sixpence pieces were added. When their turn came to stir the pudding with a big wooden spoon, the children each made a secret wish for what they wanted on Christmas Day. Eva, Vera, Phil and Hilda, cleaned the left over pudding mixture from the sides of the pan with their fingers.

Bath night in front of a coal fire.

Perhaps you, like myself, have happy recollections of doing the same.

'If I wished for something inexpensive it mostly came true', said Eva, 'if not, Mam would say I hadn't stirred the pudding hard enough'.

Because of frequent asthma attacks, and in order for the continual wheezing not to disturb the other children, Eva had a bedroom all to herself. She could just manage to make out through a crack in the rafters what was going on in the living room below. On Christmas Eve, Vera, Phil and Hilda, would tiptoe into her bedroom to see what gifts were being put in their stockings. Phil on one occasion, waited for his parents to go to bed, then crept downstairs to pinch some shoenuts. Afraid of disturbing his parents, by opening the drawer, where the nut cracker was kept, he cracked a nut between his teeth.

'Suddenly, blood spurted all over the bedclothes. The hard shell split his lip open and we couldn't stop it bleeding. In the end we had to wake Mam and confess what Phil had been up to. Dad filled the crack up a few days later, stopping us peeping into the living room for good'.

Having asthma prevented Eva joining in strenuous games. Instead, when Vera and Hilda were racing each other in the street outside, Eva passed the time sewing items for her sisters. The only game she can remember taking part in was hop scotch. Her job was chalking out an oblong and dividing it into eight numbered squares, into which a flat stone was skilfully manoevured by the contender hopping on one foot. She also drew the catherine wheel for London Scotch, in which, the squares got smaller and smaller as one reached the square marked HOME.

'It was nice to be included but far nicer to be hopping round and round the circle like the others', said Eva.

Years later Eva kept the Dynevor Arms on Swansea Road, Merthyr where beer was 1/- a pint and where in her later days 'Jones the Song' before he became world famous, was engaged as one of the turns on concert night.

Eva is quite a character with a wonderful sense of humour even though she finds it a problem to get from A to B with her Zimmer. It's nice to know she's happy in Tegfan her new home.

Eva Augusta Powell

Annie Gwen While
born 20th October, 1908

Annie Gwen, beside being the youngest of two girls and one boy, was the delicate one of the family. Their family doctor strongly suspected from certain signs and symptoms, that 5 year old, Annie Gwen, may be suffering from tuberculosis.

Her mother realised that owing to the nature of her daughter's illness she wouldn't be allowed to attend the village school like her brother and sister. The Marshall Open Air School near Aberdare Park came highly recommended for delicate children, so at seven years old, Annie Gwen was accepted as a day pupil.

'Getting to school every morning meant me catching the early train from Cwmbach village as far as Aberaman. Fortunately for me, one of the teachers caught the same tram each morning and we were able to keep each other company all the way to school', said Annie May.

Parents were required to pay a daily fee, if a child attended Marshall Open Air School. Beside being taught the approved curriculum, there were other benefits included in the fee. Nourishing drinks were supplied at both morning and afternoon breaks, as well as a well balanced meal at lunch time. The thirty pupils attending, were placed into one of three classrooms, depending on age plus tuition received up to the time of entrance. The teaching staff were used to dealing with minor problems that usually arise among delicate children, but in case of emergencies, a registered nurse was also employed on a regular basis.

During fine weather, lessons were held outside in the open air. Time was set aside for exercises, but Nurse refused to let Annie Gwen climb ladders or the parallel bars, fearing the child would strain her heart.

A substantial meal with 'afters' of rice, tapioca or semolina pudding made from goats' milk, followed when morning sessions were ended. After lunch, the pupils retired to bed for an hour, then continued the lessons until it was time to catch the tram home. Although far from well, Annie Gwen, who had a lovely voice, was among the first to stand up, when the Minister of Carmel Chapel, wanted volunteers for a forth coming concert.

The little girl could be heard, but the row of deacons in the front pew hid her completely from the audience. This situation was quickly righted by placing a high stool near the organ, where everyone could see her. Annie Gwen, was lifted onto the high stool, and held firmly by a deacon standing either side, to prevent the little girl toppling off.

'I sang lots of popular ballads', Annie said, 'but the piece that went down best and got the most encores was a popular ballad of the day entitled, 'O Where is my Wandering Boy Tonight?''

One day, not long after the social evening at Carmel Chapel, Annie Gwen was taken seriously ill. Their doctor was speedily summoned, and after a thorough examination, admitted her to Pontsarn Sanatorium on the outskirts of Merthyr.

'For six weeks no-one was allowed to visit because I was so ill. Once I was off the danger list, my mother and brother Merlin, came twice a week to see me, walking all the way from our home in Cwmbach. I doubt very much if anyone these days would consider making the long lonely journey across Aberdare Mountain into Georgestown, Merthyr and from there to Pontsarn. Rain, hail or sunshine, they managed somehow to visit me at least once a week. One year during a severe blizzard when it snowed heavily for days, I knew there'd be no visitors until the snow cleared. Believe it or not, but on the next Saturday, mother and Merlin arrived as usual. My uncle, after much deliberation, and tearful pleading from his sister, forced his horse and cab through appalling conditions along what is now called, The Heads of the Valleys Road, not to disappoint me.'

Some patients had single cubicles but Anne shared a double cubicle with an elderly lady named Sarah, who was cheerful and never stopped talking. Sarah taught the little girl to say a prayer before going to sleep each night, a prayer, which years later, Annie Gwen, taught her own children.

'If I shut my eyes I can hear Sarah saying the prayer over and over again while I repeated her words parrot fashion.'

Lord keep me safe this night, Secure from all my fears,
May angels guard me while I sleep, 'til morning light appears.

Amen

Pontsarn Sanitorium   *Courtesy: Dr. Joseph Gross*

'Sarah was a lovely lady, and her companionship helped the days pass a little quicker, The Sanatorium windows were never closed because the Health Inspector and doctors said,

'Fresh air will help kill germs quicker'.

'Believe me, we certainly had plenty of fresh air. The blustery March winds blew relentlessly across the Bryniau heading straight for our open cubicles. Sometimes it was so windy we wore our coats, caps and scarves in bed, otherewise we'd have frozen stiff in no time. Visitors were also warned to wrap up warm as ward heating would help increase the germs. In the coldest months, they sat beside the beds, wrapped up like Eskimos and looked chilled to the marrow.

Only the cubicles and wards were minus heating, other rooms such as the kitchen, doctors' room, and staff living quarters, were heated

A night at the Musical Hall.

throughout the Winter. It's surprising how quickly our bodies adjusted themselves to extreme cold, for years afterwards, even the bitterest of conditions had little effect on me'.

Both doctors and nurses at the sanatorium were kind to Annie Gwen. One doctor who came once a week to check the patients, held a special place in her heart. The twelve year old girl, would wait patiently near the fence, for his horse and carriage to drive into the grounds.

'Jump in', he'd shout.

Taking the outstretched hand, Annie Gwen still a little shaky on her feet would get into the cab longside Doctor Ernie Ward.

'Hold tight, we'll have a quick ride up the road'.

How the young girl looked forward to the half a mile outing each week, more so because Matron wouldn't allow patients further than the fence.

'You'll be able to go home for good this weekend, Annie Gwen', she was told, after the doctor's monthly check-up.

'But I don't want to go home', she replied, 'this is my home now'.

When her uncle came in his horse and cab to fetch Annie Gwen, on the following Monday morning, she changed her mind and couldn't get home fast enough.

Relatives and friends hardly recognised her, after so many years away from Cwmbach.

'They cried and hugged me and brought little gifts to welcome me home. In the end, it seemed that everybody was laughing and crying at the same time, it was really lovely to know they'd missed me.'

Through the long months of convalescence, Annie Gwen made excellent progress and resumed her interest in chapel concerts and community life in general.

'Your daughter should have her voice properly trained', said the choir master. 'She has the makings of a fine singer'.

The advice was taken to heart and Annie Gwen was sent to a well known singing teacher for special voice training. From the first lesson, he was quick in recognising the young girl's potential, and suggested she went to a certain Professor Howells who was highly qualified. After many months of tuition, Annie Gwen, becoming a soloist soprano, and sang in concert halls, auditoriums, music halls and of course in Carmel Chapel.

'Many years before this wonderful new home was ever thought of, I was requested time after time to entertain the residents living in the old Workhouse, the name we used to call it then. Yes indeed, whenever they called, I would come running, sadly remembering the days, when I myself would have given my right arm to hear a ballad or hymn sung in Welsh. My repertoire invariably included, 'Open the Gates of the Temple', because the words had a message of hope.'

A lot of change had taken place since those days. Little did Annie Gwen know then, that on October 13th 1992, she would enter the newly built Tegfan as a resident.

'What nicer companions could I find than these surrounding me?', said blind Annie Gwen.

I guided her slowly back to her chair. Feeling for the arms, she sat down before continuing.

'Or what better care could I have anywhere in the world than the care and attention I receive from every member of the staff at Tegfan'.

And I say, Amen to that.

Annie Gwen While

Ronald Cecil Rosser
born 23rd April, 1913

Ron, one of three boys, was born to an invalid mother the year before the Great War. His father was a Master Builder by profession and built both the original Woolworths and Smiths Bookshop in Aberdare town. A few weeks after Ron was born, while working on The George Hotel, his father slipped, fracturing three ribs. This caused great calamity in the smooth running household, it being quite impossible for Mrs. Prosser in her sick condition, to care for both boys then stay up half the night with baby Ron.

'Apparently, my father was at his wits' end wondering how to carry out the duties he'd undertaken to alleviate mother's burdens. Once work was over for the day, he set about doing the tasks mother was unable to complete. Jobs like soaking napkins, bathing me, putting me upstairs in the cot, and seeing to my needs throughout the night. Dad was also a sidesman in the church. Every Sunday, during the evening service, he passed the black velvet collection bag along the pews. The minister of our church and Dad were big friends and he was the one who volunteered to change my nappies and see to my feeds, during the night. When Dad's ribs began to mend, the minister still called in regularly, in case there was something he could do to help. He was a real Christian, not like those all Gas and Gaiters types, who make big promises, then conveniently forget to carry them out'.

Whenever I discussed the kind of food eaten at different meals over fifty years ago, except for a slight variation, everyone appeared to eat the same uninteresting diet of toast, broth, vegetables, swilled down by a mug of powdery cocoa. And so it was with the Prosser family. Home made bread toasted in front of the kitchen fire, was given to the three boys before they started off for school. Potato broth, or vegetables mixed with scraps of meat was waiting on the table, when they arrived home at dinner time. At teatime, it was usually, bread and dripping, and before going to bed, a mug of dark, powdery cocoa.

Ron went to the National Church School at Aberdare and was given the job of guarding the cloakroom against pieces of chewing gum. The boys stuck half chewed gum under the pegs in the cloakroom, but Ron was a keen detective and knew exactly who the culprits were by their furtive actions. Sometimes if a boy out-smarted him, which was very rare, Ron would carefully remove the gum with a pen knife. One day, a new master caught Ron copying from a class-mate and ordered the lad to report to J.C. Poole the Headmaster.

'It was a waste of time sending a boy upstairs for punishment because he'd never arrive there', laughed Ron 'specially if the teacher was new and greener than grass. Bertie Rees, had discovered a foolproof method of dodging the cane, without arousing our teacher's suspicions. The stairs leading to Sir's office, had a rough ledge running the length of the handrail. By rubbing both hands hard along the ledge, nasty red weals, similar to receiving three of the best, appeared like magic. Mind you', added Ron, 'it may have been a walk-over when a teacher was new, but our older masters were not fooled so easily'.

The three brothers had special assignments when school was over. Ron's task was cleaning cutlery which he absolutely loathed because the Brasso sent funny sensations almost like pins and needles through his fingers. As their mother's health deteriorated, there were more and more chores waiting for the boys to do when they arrived home each afternoon. Hard jobs like using the dolly to get sheets, blankets, tablecloths and white sheets clean, were done by their father.

'It was an education to watch Dad thumping the dolly up and down in the tub. No washer woman could have got the sheets whiter.'

Ron took over the ironing, which was a never ending job and shunned by both his brothers. The stack of starched shirts in the clothes basket, had to be damped down and rolled tight, before Ron was able to press out the creases with a flat iron.

'I was expert at putting the crease in trouser legs, and Dad wouldn't trust anyone but me with his best trousers, not even the lady who came later to help out'.

The brothers attended Church three times on a Sunday but Ron decided on St. John's for two special reasons. First and foremost was the big conker tree standing in the churchyard. The second reason was due to a story passed down via the grapevine, that in St. John's graveyard, a corpse had been buried in an upright position.

The conker tree was without doubt, the biggest in Aberdare, and Ron used to soak the conkers overnight in vinegar, to toughen them ready for conker competitions. As for the body buried in a standing atitude, I did a thorough research on past burials at St. John's Church and found that in 1789 a certain Quaker named David William Watkins of Aberaman had requested that his body be buried perpendiculary. As one enters the West door of St. John's, a tablet immediately to the left, records the burial and this curious request. Whether David William Watkins was so buried within the wall, or in the ground in a standing position or on the other hand buried in the normal way vertically below the tablet, remains unsolved. Legend has it, that David William Watkins had a servant by the name of Shoni Mawr, who from all accounts, was a giant of a man. Being unable to look down upon his servant in life, the Quaker wanted to be sure of looking down on Shoni in death. Sadly the inscription on the tablet is rapidly crumbling and very soon the story of this curious burial will exist only in written history.

A game played with a small piece of wood sharpened either end, then bounced along the road with a larger stick, was popular with both men and boys back there. The game was known by different names depending on where one happened to live, but Ron referred to it as, 'Dog and Cat'. George Hanney's illustration on the next page, clarifies the game.

Men
Playing
Cat and Dog

Cartoon by George Hanney

'Most of my friends had iron hoops, but mine had a special ring on the end to stop anyone running off with it', said Ron. 'I was also a crackhand at marbles, and won a collection of both glasses and china Tors, from older competitors.

One of his uncles named Lew, started the first charabanc service in Aberdare. On Bank Holiday Monday, the pavement in front of Woolworths, would be crowded with families, hoping to get on the charabanc for a day trip to Penderyn or Ystradfellte.

A trip from Penderyn to Ystradfellte.

Another trip by charabanc in the good old Summertime.

'I must have been about eight years old when we went to Pembroke for our holidays. The only thing I remember about the town, was narrow cobbled streets and quaint houses. We stayed on a farm a few miles outside the town itself, and used to help the farmer's wife feed the geese, ducks and chickens before having our breakfast. The farmer gave us permission to play in the farmyard as long as we didn't get up to any mischief. By lunch time I was whacked out and usually looked for a quiet spot to eat my sandwiches. One particular day, going into a field, I noticed a wagon loaded with hay. Climbing up the wooden sides, I dropped down onto the warm soft hay and fell asleep. When I awoke, my body was damp and the foul smell coming from my clothes, made me sick. I was covered in manure. How was I too know what lay under the top layer of freshly cut hay? All I know, it took hours to get rid of the evil smelling manure from my hair and for days afterwards the horrid odour remained in my nostrils. The farmer, roared with laughter when he saw me'.

'That will teach you to look before you leap lad', he said, thumping me on the back.

At thirteen, Ron was confirmed by the Bishop of Llandaff but being a firm believer that variety is the spice of life, he went wherever there were free concerts or magic lantern shows. Most magic lantern slides depicted well known bible stories, such as Moses in the bullrushes, the flood of Noah's day, or the Ten Commandments. Later on Ron joined the Boy Scouts, but after buying his cap and whistle and perfecting a clove hitch knot, he decided to quit.

'Did you not enjoy singing around the camp fire?', I inquired.

'I didn't last that long', said Ron 'beside, whenever the Scout Master planned a weekend in the country, it rained buckets and our tents were awash'.

As he grew older Ron changed his teatime routine of bread and dripping to the luxury of a tasty kipper cooked slowly on an iron grid over the kitchen fire. When the kipper was done to a turn, Ron sat at the table for the biggest part of the evening removing hundreds of tiny bones.

There was a stall in Aberdare Market with a fresh fish slab, where any kippers left over at the end of the day were sold for two pennies each. With no deep freezers to store perishable food, the stall holders were also glad to get rid of unsold fruit for a few coppers and Ron remembers buying a full stalk of bananas for sixpence. We named the outside market, 'Jerusalem', because the majority of stall owners were Jews.

'I can still hear the bushy bearded old Jew calling out to men in the crowd'.

'Don't go avay, don't go avay, come see vhat I have vor the vife'. He'd wave a pair of red flannel bloomers with one hand and some very naughty underwear with the other.

Another character named Maggie Faggots, had a faggott and peas booth inside the market, where you could either eat a meal on the premises or carry the faggots and peas home in your basin.

'Nothing is the same since my wife passed away', sighed Ron. 'That's why I had to come to Tegfan, I'm lucky to have a nice room of my own and do my best to keep active and cheerful'.

Ronald Cecil Rosser

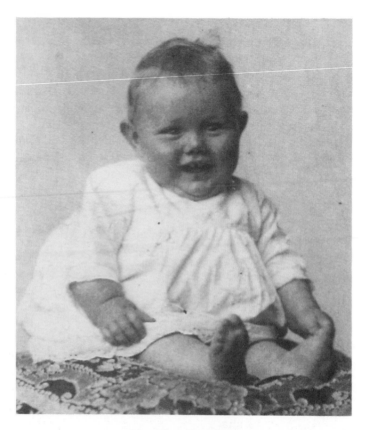

Emily Cunvil

born 9th February, 1913

Emily was the youngest but one of seven sisters brought up in a happy and loving environment, at their family home in Gadlys Row. All the children attended the Board School in Monk Street until the day Emily came home with her pinafore almost ripped apart.

'Tell me who did it, we'll go straight to the girl's house', demanded her mother.

'Teacher', replied Emily bursting into floods of tears.

Her mother was furious, not just because a teacher of all people was the culprit but making pinafores cost hours of precious time with seven daughters to cook, wash, mend and care for. The following morning, the girls in support of their sister, lined up outside the room marked Headmistress. Meanwhile, their mother paced backward and forward along the corridor like an angry tigress, until she was called into the office.

'I want the whole story, exactly what happened, Emily, with nothing added or taken away', said the Headmistress sternly.

'Miss Evans was writing on the board when the chalk suddenly snapped in two. I began to giggle like the rest of the class. Miss Evans turned round, looked straight at me, and said I was making fun of her. It was untrue, I never made fun of her. Catching my pinny, she dragged me out in front of the class and shook me until I felt sick'.

'She shook you as well did she, you didn't mention that before.'

By this time Mam was breathing fire, and our Headmistress looked scared to death.

'I demand that my girls be transferred immediately to the Mardy School, otherwise I'm going to the police station', threatened Mrs. Dix, shaking her fist in temper.

That same day, seven new names were entered on the pupils' register at the Mardy School. The children felt very embarrassed when their classmates asked the reason for the sudden change of schools. Like any other seven day wonder, the episode was quickly forgotten, and the sisters settled down without further problems.

'My job after school was cleaning the outside toilet. I hated it enough to hand over my share of sweets to whoever did it instead of me. Giving away my sweets was a real sacrifice as none of us had money to go to the shop and buy more. I got away with it for a long time. Then Mammy caught my sister Elsie scrubbing the toilet seat and smacked my bum with the 'Ginny', until it smarted too much to sit down. Having my full share of sweets once more, helped soften the blow a little, but even when toilets were installed indoors and easy to clean I still hated the job.'

Frederick Dix took his seven daughters to a small Church Mission each Sunday without fail, come hail, rain or shine. It was customary in the Mission, for young people wishing to become members, to be confirmed at twelve years of age. When the time arrived, Emily, like her sisters, was confirmed at St. Elvans Church.

'My mother used iron saucepans to cook the vegetables, and a bakestone to cook Welshcakes or blackberry turnover on our coal fire. All other baking was done in the oven, even the big loaf cakes on Christmas. Like everyone else, Mammy washed our changes once a week in the tub, and used a heavy flat iron heated between the fire bars, to press the clothes. We had family members who were real Aunties, and loads of so called Aunties who were no relation to Mammy or Daddy. One such person known as Auntie May, used to take a Sunday School class of about twenty children. When class was over, we'd wait for Auntie May outside the Mission. Thinking nothing of it, she'd take the twenty or more of us, for a bracing ramble up the Cwm. We all loved her very much. One afternoon, I asked why she took us for walks, her answer was as follows.

'It does me a power of good to be with young people, but most of all it gives your mothers a well deserved break for a few hours.'

Emily liked playing cricket with the boys, but first she had to collect yeast from the bakehouse and gather nettles from the hedgerows for her mother to make small beer. There was still another job to do before the little girl was free to play outside, washing and drying a load of empty pop flagons in readiness for the small beer. Sometimes her mother needed help to cork the bottles tightly and carry them to the stone shelf in their pantry. By this time, Emily would be too tired to play. The flagons were sold for 4d each, to help supplement her father's wages of £3.5s, which had to support a family of nine.

'Sometimes the pop, pop, pop, of corks hitting the pantry ceiling when the small beer was ready, woke us up from our sleep. We'd creep quietly downstairs to the pantry and watch the small beer rise in a pillar of froth, above the bottle tops'.

On Guy Fawkes afternoon, seats borrowed from the Mission were placed in a circle around the pile of sticks and old rubbish ready for the sing-song. Later on, the miners brought their block and bits of coal to get the bonfire going and residents sang and danced until the embers died away.

Emily remembers the time when half a dozen Aberdare men went to fight in the Spanish Civil War, mainly because Tom Howel Jones came from Monk Street. She also recalls joining the crowd at Aberaman railway station when some survivors returned.

'It was just before Christmas when we heard that five out of the six men were alive and coming home. Poor Tom was killed by a shell fragment and buried in the Spanish hills. A few days later a welcome back meeting was held at Aberdare Centre of Unemployment. Everyone cried when one of the survivors called Edwin Greening, said that Tom had died in his arms and his comrades laid him to rest in an almond grove'.

Mrs. Dix, Emily's grandmother, was one of the oldest of 150 residents living on the Cwm. There was a public house, a mission hut, a row of houses on top of the hill called Pont Flash and a halt where the G.W.R. train, driven by a character called Mexican Joe, picked up anyone going to town.

No-one seems to know how it came about, but the house where Mrs. Dix resided was built on a public right of way, and many of the scattered dwellings were only accessible by walking through her

A day at the seaside.

house.

'People would be knocking the door from morn 'till night, but Grandma didn't seem to mind, she'd laugh and say',

'How many coconut matting already have you worn out for me'. When Mrs. Dix became blind, she knew by the person's knock, who was outside waiting to walk through her house.

Mr. and Mrs. Dix, took their daughters to Barry Island once a year while the children played sand castles on the beach, their parents sat listening to the Salvation Army band. Being nine in number, they found it too expensive to have a meal in the big restaurant facing the sands called the 'Merrie Friars'. Instead, before leaving home early that morning, enough meat paste sandwiches to last throughout the day, were packed in a brown paper carrier. The girls carried their own buckets and spades, and took turns with the bag holding two flagons of small beer.

'Tired out, we'd sit on the sands and sing along with the Salvation Army band until the sun went down and it was time to catch the train back home', said Emily. 'As you grow older, all you really need is a clean bed, three meals a day and someone to love you. I've got all this at Tegfan, plus no gas, electric, water or poll tax bills to worry about. The important thing is to learn to adapt yourself. If you can do that, you'll find peace, contentment and true companionship.'

Emily Cunvil

The Chef at Tegfan adding his story to the Workshop group.

Staff of Tegfan.

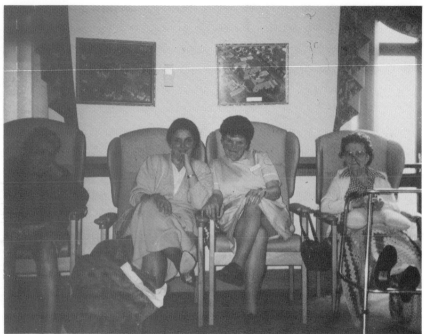

Quiet moments at Tegfan.

Tea break before recommencing our Workshop.

Ron, myself, Emily and Albert checking notes.

Tea's up at 4 p.m.

Acknowledgements

First and foremost, my sincere thanks to Bob Mole of the South East Wales Arts Association for his help and encouragement to set up workshops in five Residential Homes, where a wealth of experiences gathered from the older residents incited me to pen the most informative recollections for posterity. Also a big Thank You to Mr. G. Williams, Director of Social Services for supporting the workshops, and South East Wales Arts Association for supporting the publication of my book.

Secondly, I say, Thank You, to the ever young at heart residents whose enthralling and vivid memories of a past era has made 'Remember When' a compilation worthy of publication.

I'd like to acknowledge Officers Marilyn Bracegirdle, Heather Paul, Margo Pugh, Mary Williams and the staff of Llysfaen, Sandbrook, Victoria and the Gurnos Residential Homes for their willing help and kind assistance during my workshops.

I thank Mr. Geoffrey Hanney for giving permission to use a number of his father's cartoons. His father, the late George Hanney, was a well known artist and cartoonist extraordinare. His hilarious illustration entitled 'The Bun Fight', which I chose to grace the cover of 'Remember When', seemed exactly right to sum up the innocent fun of a passing generation.

I am also grateful to, Mrs. Maisie Gough of Cefn Coed, for relating the history of her grandmother, Mary Elin, who farmed the land on which Llysfaen Residential Home now stands. The other people I'd like to thank are Mrs. Eirwen McDonald of Tudor Street, Merthyr for describing life at Brynteg House before it became Sandbrook House Rheumatic Hospital. Mrs. Betty Thomas for a wealth of informative material on village life in Cefn Coed. Also Mr. Owen Williams of Nelson for relating the pitfalls of being an errand boy.

I certainly shall not forget the help I received during hours of research from, Carolyn Jacob, our Reference Librarian at Merthyr Central Library or the willingness of Libraries Officer, Geraint James, for co-operating in every possible way.

I end my acknowledgements by thanking Mr. Andrew Owen for the wonderful job he did on copying the many photos donated by families, friends, libraries and some very special prints loaned to me by Bill Jones BA, PhD of the Welsh Industrial and Maritime Museum.

Indeed, Mr. Andrew Owen was able by his expertise, to improve the quality of damaged and faded snapshots to such an extent, that every photograph however old, was good enough to use.

My Thanks to You All.

Iris Roderick Thomas